PICTORIAL HISTORY OF
THE US AIR FORCE

PICTORIAL HISTORY
OF THE
US AIR FORCE

DAVID MONDEY

LONDON

IAN ALLAN

First published 1971

This enlarged paperback edition first published 1974

ISBN 0 7110 0508 7

*Published by Ian Allan Ltd, Shepperton, Surrey and printed in Great
Britain by Morrison and Gibb Ltd, London and Edinburgh*

Contents

Foreword

by COL. JOHN W. KEELER, USAF

Director of Information, Headquarters Air Training Command

FEW aviation historians have ventured outside their national boundaries to write a history on a foreign air force. David Mondey is one of the few and must be commended for his work.

For twenty-eight years I have been a part of the great, growing force which Mr. Mondey has chronicled. I am proud and honored that a "foreigner" has taken the time and effort to research and compile this *Pictorial History of the United States Air Force*.

The 1960's have been termed the most action-packed era in American aviation history. To fully appreciate the technical strides of this brief decade, a person should re-examine the exciting feats of half a century before it. This chronicle does just that—blending the heroic adventures and advances into perspective. I commend it to all who share a sincere interest in airplanes and space exploration.

End and Beginning

As TWILIGHT gave way to night, on December 17, 1903, there ended a day that marks one of history's milestones. On that day, at Kill Devil Hill, near Kitty Hawk, North Carolina, Orville and Wilbur Wright had, with their optimistically-named aircraft—the Flyer—made the first-ever powered, sustained and almost-controlled flight.

Their achievement marked the end of the long experimental period in which man had sought to emulate the birds. Powered flight was an accomplished fact. Ahead lay only technical improvement. It was an end.

It was also a beginning. Amongst other things the Wrights provided some of the earliest material for those writers who, today, seek to gain somewhat dubious fame by disparaging those who can no longer defend themselves. They have said that this achievement by two uneducated bicycle mechanics was nothing more than a fluke; that they had merely wedded the glider of Lilienthal with the internal combustion engine perfected by Daimler.

In truth, it marked a beginning of scientific application to the problems of powered flight. It seemed, too, to mark the beginning of a golden age of travel, but within a mere fifteen years, at the end of World War I, when the potential of military aviation could be appreciated by even the most naïve observer, a disillusioned Orville Wright commented: "What a dream it was; what a nightmare it has become."

Nevertheless, for good or evil, the Wrights provided the beginning of that vast aerial armada that we know today as the United States Air Force.

The writer hopes that this very condensed history of the USAF may give the reader some appreciation of its aims—another end and beginning —an end of global war, the beginning of lasting peace.

D. C. M.

July 1970.

Acknowledgements

ACKNOWLEDGEMENT is, to me, a rather severe word. It seems more akin to the commercial formality of Dickensian times and unsuited to express appreciation. So, I would offer my sincere gratitude to John W. R. Taylor, editor of *Jane's All the World's Aircraft*, for his generous advice and encouragement; to John Dennison, historian of the US 3rd Air Force, who has not only given unstinted help, but has also checked the historical accuracy of my script and made innumerable suggestions for its improvement; and to Lewis Nalls of Alexandria, Virginia, who was responsible for extracting from USAF files the superb pictures that make this a "pictorial" history. Last, but by no means least, a sincere thank-you to Colonel John Keeler, USAF, for his generous foreword.

The illustrations in the last sixteen pages came from John W. R. Taylor, T. Matsuzaki, Gordon S. Williams, Stephen P. Peltz, The Singer Company, Air Portraits and Brian M. Service, but the majority are USAF official photographs and I am most grateful for permission to use them: as well as to Thomas Y. Crowell and Company of New York to quote from Chelsea Fraser's *Heroes of the Air*; Laurence Pollinger Ltd of London and Appleton-Century-Crofts of New York for the quotation from Quentin Reynolds' *The Amazing Mr Doolittle*.

Two's Company

Two is company: three is none
19th century proverb

ON AUGUST 1, 1907, the Signal Corps of the United States Army established an Aeronautical Division, to be responsible for "all matters pertaining to military ballooning, air machines and all kindred objects". It was not exactly a vast division, consisting of but three men: Cpl. Edward Ward and First-Class Private Joseph E. Barrett, under the command of Capt. Charles de F. Chandler. When, a short time later—and possibly influenced by the proverb quoted above—Private Barrett went "AWOL", the Army's air arm lost fifty per cent of its enlisted strength.

This seemingly-late formation date of the Aeronautical Division may be surprising, having regard to the fact that the first powered flight had taken place almost three and a half years earlier. This was due, chiefly, to exaggerated accounts and poor reporting, which resulted in the achievement of the Wrights being neither appreciated nor believed, not only by the United States government but by the world at large. Furthermore, an earlier attempt to sponsor heavier-than-air flight had caused the Army no little embarrassment.

In 1896, Professor S. P. Langley had flown successfully a 14-foot span steam-powered model aeroplane which he called an "Aerodrome". The US Army, prompted by General Greely and other officers, had provided Langley with a sum of $50,000 to build a full-size version. When it failed to fly—both attempts terminating in disaster when the aircraft hit a post on the launching gear—Congress and public alike criticised the Army severely for squandering public money on such a ridiculous invention.

With their fingers once burned, it was not surprising that the Board of Ordnance and Fortification, responsible for investigating new military equipment, declined to part with any money when the Wrights twice offered their invention to the US Army in 1905. In fact, not only did they doubt the existence of the aeroplane, they were so sensitive to possible misinterpretation of their own actions that they would not even state their performance requirements for a military aircraft when the Wrights asked for this information, towards the end of October 1905.

This was rather more than ironical, for on October 5 Flyer No. 3 had covered a distance of 24·2 miles in a time of 38 minutes 3 seconds.

It was almost two years later that the War Department, conscious of the progress of military aviation in Europe and concerned that the United States was falling too far behind, decided to invite bids for an aircraft on December 23, 1907. This was required to carry two persons at a speed of 40 mph over a distance of 125 miles. Three bids were received and approved on February 8, 1908. In the event, only the Wright machine was delivered, at a contract price of $25,000, which provided also for the tuition of two pilots.

The aircraft which the Wrights produced to meet the Army's requirements was a modification of their 1905 Flyer, powered by a 30 hp engine and able to carry two persons. Like the earlier models it had skid landing gear and was launched from a monorail track. They delivered the aircraft to Fort Myer, Virginia, and demonstration flights were made from September 3, 1908. People came in their thousands to watch, were thrilled by the miracle of powered flight and, for the first time, realised that the Wrights' claims had been in no measure exaggerated.

Unfortunately, within a fortnight the flights came to a tragic end: the aircraft crashed and Orville Wright was injured severely, his passenger, Lt. Thomas E. Selfridge, was killed.

It was not until June 1909 that the Wrights delivered an improved version of their 1908 machine to Fort Myer where, on July 27, Orville Wright with Lt. Frank P. Lahm as passenger, established a world record duration for a two-man flight of 1 hour, 12 minutes, 40 seconds. On August 2 the Army accepted this aircraft, which the Washington *Star* recorded as "Aeroplane No. 1, Heavier-than-air Division, United States Aerial Fleet". More accurately, it was Signal Corps aircraft No. 1.

With the nucleus of an air arm, the Army's next requirement was for pilots to fly it. Under the contract, Orville Wright duly gave instruction to Lt. Lahm and Lt. Frederic E. Humphreys, and both had achieved solo flights by October 26. Within ten days the new air force was back at square one, when Lahm and Humphreys crashed "No. 1", and shortly afterwards these pilots, too, had gone, returned to their regular service commitments.

While the aircraft was being repaired, the Army decided to move its flying centre to Fort Sam Houston, Texas, for the winter, as this area promised better flying conditions.

The only remaining officer on flying duty, Lt. Benjamin D. Foulois—later to become Chief of the United States Air Service overseas in World War I—was responsible for packing the repaired aircraft for transit to Texas, where he arrived in February 1910. By March 2 "No. 1" was ready for flight, and Foulois took on the responsibility of becoming its pilot, the Wrights sending him flying instructions by mail, plus an instructor to help master the tricky problem of landing. He learnt well: between March and September he made 61 flights, and had the distinction of being the only pilot of the Army's only aircraft.

Early in 1911, and not a moment too soon, a Wright Type 8 aeroplane was loaned to the Signal Corps by the publisher, Robert F. Collier, for on May 4 the fast-aging "No. 1" was retired from service and, after restoration, put on permanent exhibition in the Smithsonian Institution.

At that time, lack of enthusiasm for military aviation in America, plus the struggle for finance, paralleled the experiences of the Balloon Section of the Royal Engineers in Great Britain. By the beginning of 1911, for example, US Congress had not allocated a single cent of finance for military aviation and the Signal Corps fought a losing battle in its attempts to get an appropriation for its aviation activities of $200,000 a year. Typical of Congressional reaction was the reported comment: "Why all this fuss about airplanes for the Army? I thought we already had one."

But the turning point was at hand: in March 1911 Congress finally relented with an appropriation of $125,000. Of this sum, $25,000 was to be available immediately, and Chief Signal Officer James Allen at once ordered five new aircraft, one of which was the first military type Model D Curtiss biplane with pusher engine, and which became Signal Corps aircraft No. 2. Its builder, Glenn L. Curtiss, who had started the first aeroplane manufacturing company in the United States, was also one of America's pioneer flyers. He established a small flying school on North Island, San Diego Bay, during the winter of 1910–11—subsequently to become the Army's first permanent aviation school—and he invited the Army and Navy to send officers for free flying instruction.

The first three selected for training, in January 1911, were all Army officers: Lts. Paul W. Beck, G. E. M. Kelly and John C. Walker, Jnr. In April they joined Foulois at Fort Sam Houston where, on May 10, the first fatality in flying training occurred when Lt. Kelly was killed trying to crash-land his Curtiss pusher in order to avoid troops engaged on manoeuvres. This resulted in the commanding general forbidding any further flying activities at the Fort.

This could have been yet another setback for the struggling air force if construction of a flying school at College Park, near Washington, DC, had not already begun. The pilots and aircraft moved to their new school during June and July and flying was resumed as quickly as possible. Foulois was posted for duty in Washington and Capt. Chandler, once again chief of the Aeronautical Division, became commandant at College Park.

At this time the Army had no official qualification tests for a pilot, and so adopted the regulations of the *Fédération Aeronautique Internationale*

(FAI). Among the first of the early entrants to qualify as a pilot was one Lt. Henry H. ("Hap") Arnold, a man who was to have tremendous influence on the USAF of the future. Together with Lt. T. D. Milling, he had been trained at Simms Station, Dayton, Ohio, and these two were the first Wright School Army pilots.

Availability of funds was reflected in the expansion of aviation activities during 1911 and 1912. Among the achievements was a 42-mile cross-country flight, a record-breaking altitude flight of 4,674 ft made by Lt. Arnold, experiments in aerial photography and night flying, as well as early flight tests of bomb-sights and machine-guns, and the first co-ordinated manoeuvres with ground troops were held during August 1912.

By November 1912, College Park school numbered fourteen flying officers, 39 enlisted men and nine aircraft, including hydroplanes, and for the first time it seemed that the force had acquired some stability, with steady expansion but a matter of time.

In order to gain this sort of stability, a general order had been issued on May 27, 1912, providing official recognition for pilots by the intro-duction of the rating of Military Aviator. Those who qualified—a total of 24 officers—were entitled to wear a specially designed badge, receiving also a Military Aviator's Certificate. A year later, to enhance the position still further, Congress authorised 35 per cent extra pay for a maximum of thirty officers regularly assigned to flying duties.

Despite these attempts to make conditions more attractive to its pilots, morale was dangerously low in the spring of 1913, due to lack of confi-dence in their leadership, added to a high accident rate. Pilots of the 1st Aero Squadron, a provisional unit operating with the 2nd Division at Texas City, sent a round-robin letter to the Chief Signal Officer, Brig. Gen. George P. Scriven, voicing their complaints. This was but the first of a series of incidents that led to the Army's pilots being considered as temperamental as a bunch of film stars, and later being described as: "deficient in discipline and the proper knowledge of the customs of the service and the duties of an officer". Their prime demand was to have commanders with flying experience and it was this factor, above all others, that eventually gained autonomy for the air force.

Another important decision at the end of 1913 brought closure of College Park school and the designation of North Island as the Signal Corps Aviation School where, for the first time, the curriculum included the study of related subjects such as engineering, science and meteorology.

At the beginning of 1914, therefore, when the thunderheads of war were piling up over Europe, the United States could at least congratulate herself with the thought that, at last, her air arm was reasonably well established. That was about the limit of her satisfaction. There was no doubt that she was trailing far behind Europe in military aviation. Her aircraft industry was only just beginning to emerge from the stage of experimental and freakish design. Her aero-engine industry was virtually non-existent. Congress had provided but a mere pittance with which to attempt the creation of an effective air force, even assuming there were suitable aircraft to be bought.

Not least of her problems was that of getting and keeping pilots. The high fatality rate—25 per cent of the first 48 officers assigned to flying duties—was hardly conducive to recruitment: not only did it make the War Department reluctant to detail officers to flying duties from other arms and services, it also resulted in few volunteers, because they could see no future in flying.

Paramount, however, was the real lack of motivation. There was little finance, no seemingly-essential military duties, and little interest in or appreciation of the force's achievements by higher authority. In face of such indifference it is not surprising that the Signal Corps found it increasingly difficult to maintain its air arm.

It was not until July 18, 1914, that Army aviation received statutory recognition, when Congress approved creation of the Aviation Section, Signal Corps, with Lt. Col. Samuel Reber in command of an authorised strength of 60 officers and 260 other ranks. Duties of the Aviation Section were clearly defined for the first time and this, together with better finance, resolved the major problem.

It could not, of course, overcome the deficiency in equipment. The Signal Corps made the first move by condemning all aircraft with pusher engines, for it had been aircraft of this configuration which were responsible for the majority of fatal accidents. With these out of the reckoning, there were precious few aircraft left at all: at North Island, for example, there remained only five trainers, and even these needed considerable reconditioning to be of any real use. The training programme was kept going by the purchase of a sporting plane from Glenn L. Martin of Los Angeles, this being converted into a two-seat dual-control trainer.

Fortunately, an important aeroplane was on the point of entering service: on June 24, 1914, the first Curtiss JN-1 tractor biplane (Signal Corps No. 29) was received at San Diego. It was the forerunner of a whole series of training aircraft, known affectionately as the "Jenny", which was to provide a reliable trainer for a whole generation of student pilots, military and civil alike.

One reliable type was hardly sufficient. With a somewhat odd assortment of early aircraft presenting a nightmare of maintenance, the Aviation Section thought it prudent at that time to seek a standard aeroplane able to meet their safety and performance requirements. A competition amongst aircraft manufacturers, sponsored in October 1914, produced only a single aircraft able to meet the specification of four hours' non-stop flight and a climb to 4,000 ft in ten minutes with full load. Happily it was soon realised that the speed of development of both airframes and engines would not allow standardisation of this kind, which could only result in the freezing of all attempts to experiment with new aircraft and untried techniques.

Despite its difficulties, the Aviation Section gradually grew in size and organisation. In December 1914, General Scriven called for four squadrons, each with eight aircraft, plus a 50 per cent reserve, to be manned by twenty officers and ninety other ranks per squadron. Rather less than a year later he had raised his sights to eighteen squadrons, each with twelve aircraft, but it was not until America entered World War I that Army aviation expanded on such a scale.

Meanwhile, the 1st Aero Squadron, which had retained a somewhat tenuous hold on life since its formation early in 1913, had reorganised at San Diego in September 1914 on an official basis, with a total of 16 officers, 75 other ranks and eight aircraft, under the command of Captain Foulois. Not only did it represent the whole tactical air strength of the Army; within a few months of its arrival at Fort Sam Houston in November 1915, it became the first American tactical air unit to be tested under field conditions.

On March 9, 1916, Pancho Villa, most notorious of the revolutionary leaders opposing the Carranza regime in northern Mexico, raided Columbus, New Mexico, killing 17 Americans. The US government reacted quickly to this audacious action, ordering Brig. Gen. John J. Pershing, with a force of 15,000 troops, to pursue Villa into Mexico and take him, dead or alive. The 1st Aero Squadron was ordered to Columbus in support; Capt. Foulois with eight aircraft, ten officers and 84 other ranks, arrived there on March 15: by May his squadron numbered 16 officers and 122 men.

They had little chance of success, for their frail aircraft could hardly be expected to survive operations in mountainous regions, where forced-landings were a daily hazard, and high winds, dust storms and snow storms were thrown in for good measure.

Even if they could not report success, they were able to record some adventures. For example, two aircraft landed at Chihuahua City, in Mexico, with duplicate despatches for the American consul. Capt. Foulois' aircraft received a volley of rifle fire before he was seized and thrown into gaol. The pilot of the second aircraft, Lt. Dargue, managed to avoid this treatment, but while he went to find the local Mexican commander to secure Foulois' release, a crowd surrounded the aircraft, burning holes in the wings with cigarettes, ripping the fabric-covered fuselage, and removing nuts, bolts and anything else easily portable. When Foulois was released from his prison, both aircraft managed to take off, but Lt. Dargue had to force-land almost immediately when a top section of the fuselage blew off and damaged the tailplane. He had the unpleasant task of guarding his aircraft against an aggressive mob until Mexican soldiers arrived eventually to guard the machine. Hurried repairs were made overnight, and he managed to get safely away at 5.30 am the next morning.

By April 20 only two of 1st Aero Squadron's aircraft were capable of flight, and when taken from their operating area back to Columbus they, too, were condemned and destroyed. Replacement aircraft fared no better, despite which the squadron continued to be based at Columbus until early in 1917.

The near-fiasco of the operations in Mexico did more than anything else to convince the US government of the desperate shortcomings of Army aviation. At a time when military aircraft in Europe were demonstrating daily their rugged reliability in combat, their own military aircraft seemed limited to short, peaceful flights, in good weather conditions. Their answer was to provide, in August 1916, an unprecedented sum of $13,281,666 for military aeronautics.

Unfortunately, they were closing the stable door too late. No amount of money could buy aircraft, aero-engines and equipment that were not in existence. America was not the only country to learn—the hard way —that an advanced-thinking and successful aircraft industry is sired by an equally advanced-thinking parent—that is to say, a wise government.

Whilst it was not possible to provide any revolutionary new aircraft in the short time that remained before the United States became embroiled in the European conflict, certain improvements were possible. The National Defense Act of 1916 increased the strength of the Aviation Section and provided a reserve: the Aero Club of America, which had been a driving force in organising flying enthusiasts into air units in various States, provided another important source of manpower for the Aviation Section.

The Signal Corps, with a clear view of the task ahead, made strenuous efforts to improve training facilities. By October 1916 there were 45 officers under training at San Diego; a new school was opened at Mineola, New York, training candidates for the reserve corps and National Air Guard; and a new flying school was opened at Essington, Pennsylvania. In addition, civilian flying schools began to train reservists for the Aviation Section. An early pupil of the civilian flying schools was a certain Major William ("Billy") Mitchell who, in the autumn of 1916, was assistant chief of the Aviation Section.

In 1916, the War Department gave authorisation for seven squadrons, each comprising twelve aircraft. Of these, the 1st, 3rd, 4th and 5th would be stationed in the United States, with the 2nd Squadron in the Philippines, the 6th in Hawaii and the 7th in Panama. All were in existence early in 1917.

Of these seven squadrons, only the 1st Squadron was fully organised and equipped—if equipped is a suitable word. It was with this untried and, in terms of machines, desperately weak air arm, that the United States entered the First World War—a war in which millions of men had already been locked in bloody and deadly combat for almost three years.

A Different Course

Europe has a set of primary interests which to us have none or a very remote relation. Hence she must be engaged in frequent controversies, the causes of which are essentially foreign to our concerns. . . . Our detached and distant situation invites and enables us to pursue a different course.

George Washington. Farewell Address. 1796

BY REASON OF her geographical position, it had long been comparatively easy for America to pursue a policy of isolation. Her moat was deep and wide and she was, to a large extent, self-sufficient. Only twice before 1917 had she been militarily involved in intercontinental affairs —the Spanish-American War and the Boxer Rebellion in China. Her relationship with Europe had been influenced by governmental policy of the kind expressed by George Washington in his Farewell Address to Congress and, later, by the message to Congress of James Monroe, better known as the Monroe Doctrine.

At the outbreak of World War I, America was totally unready to participate in a conflict of such magnitude and immediately declared her neutrality. Despite serious disruption of her export trade, resulting from the effective Allied blockade of Europe, this neutrality was maintained for almost three years.

There seems little doubt that, economically, America could have stayed out of the war, but sabotage by German agents, sinking of the *Lusitania* —which caused the death of 128 Americans—and increasing losses in her mercantile fleet by U-boat action, aroused intense anti-German feelings. Finally came the interception of a German despatch, promising Mexico that if she would ally herself with Germany, a victorious and gracious Kaiser would ensure the return to Mexico of territories incorporated in the United States in 1848. This was the last straw: on April 6, 1917, the United States declared war on Germany.

The war then raging in Europe was unique in its carnage and ferocity. For those who were not involved, and have no personal knowledge of its true nature, Remarque's *All Quiet on the Western Front* sketches most vividly the almost unbelievable horror: the mud, the filth, the stench of corpses—animal and human—the lice, the mind-shattering-body-numbing barrage, the chlorine gas that, at the whim of a breeze, choked friend and foe alike; the bloated rats that fed on the dead—and dying.

America was absolutely unprepared for warfare of this nature. More accurately, she was unprepared for war at all. The mere idea of planning in advance for a possible war was distasteful to the American people, completely foreign to the War Department, and even President Wilson was outraged that such a measure should be deemed necessary. It required considerable argument from the Chief of Staff and the Secretary of War to convince him otherwise.

If the Army was unversed in the art of modern war, it was hardly to be expected that its aeronautical foster-child should be any better schooled or equipped. In fact, the Aviation Section comprised 131 officers, 1,087 other ranks and fewer than 250 aeroplanes, the latter barely comparing in quality and performance with the training aircraft of the belligerent nations.

In the two months following America's entry into the war, small financial appropriations seemed to suggest that the War Department envisaged only a minor rôle for aviation. But the Allies had different views, and in May 1917 the French Premier, Alexandre Ribot, cabled President Wilson calling for an American flying corps of 4,500 aircraft, 5,000 pilots and 50,000 mechanics within a year, to give the Allies air supremacy. It was a rather tall order, for America's aircraft industry had produced fewer than 1,000 aircraft, civil and military combined, in the preceding thirteen years.

In June 1917, Foulois headed a group of officers charged with the preparation of a draft production programme. It provided for 22,625 aircraft, almost 44,000 engines, plus 80 per cent spares (equalling another 17,600 aircraft). Approved by the Secretary of War, the plan was acclaimed by press and public, who were thrilled at the idea of huge fleets of American aircraft bringing a quick end to hostilities in Europe. Brig. Gen. George O. Squier, Chief Signal Officer, was so enthusiastic that he appealed to the country to "put the Yankee punch into the war by building an army in the air, regiments and brigades of winged cavalry on gas-driven flying horses".

Such a programme needed massive finance: in July Congress rushed through an appropriation of $640 million—the largest sum for a single purpose ever voted by Congress up to that time. But money and ambitious plans were not enough. In August 1918, General Pershing and the War Department agreed on a more realistic programme, calling for 202 squadrons to be at the front by July 1, 1919, comprising 60 pursuit, 49 corps observation, 52 Army observation, 14 day bombing and 27 night bombing squadrons. In the final analysis, only 45 combat squadrons arrived at the front by the time of the Armistice.

By the spring of 1918, the high hopes of the previous year had given way to disillusionment. Instead of a flood, aircraft production was but a feeble trickle: and production was not the only problem, there were growing pains too, resulting from reorganisation of the whole structure of military aviation. On May 21, 1918, President Wilson created from the Signal Corps the Bureau of Aircraft Production and the Division of Military Aeronautics. The former, with John D. Ryan, chairman of the civilian Aircraft Board at its head, was responsible for production of aircraft, engines and equipment. The latter, under the command of Maj. Gen. William M. Kenly, controlled training and operation. Unfortunately, lack of co-ordination between these two agencies tended to outweigh the potential, and it was not until August 27 that the President resolved the problem by making Ryan Director of Air Service and Second Assistant Secretary of War.

The United States aircraft industry has often been criticised for the fact that it failed to produce the right kind of aircraft in sufficient numbers. Such criticism is hardly fair. When America declared war there were only 12 companies capable of building aircraft for the government, and during 1916 their production had totalled fewer than 400 aircraft of all kinds. They had no knowledge of the type of combat aircraft required for service in Europe, a fault for which the Allies must accept much of the blame, because prior to America's entry into the war they had exercised strict censorship of aviation matters and had refused to allow American officers to study conditions at the front.

When the Army were able to send a mission to the front in June 1917, headed by Maj. Raynal C. Bolling, it was soon decided that the best course was to concentrate on the design and construction of training aircraft and to purchase fighter aircraft from the Allies. The decision to buy rather than design fighters was realistic, having regard to the fact that the rapid development of new aircraft and new techniques would make it extremely difficult for an industry so remote from the scene of battle to keep sufficiently up-to-date.

However, the Americans did decide to build at home two British aircraft: the de Havilland DH4, a two-seat reconnaissance bomber, and the Handley Page 0/400 bomber, together with the three-engined Italian Caproni bomber. As events transpired, only the former was built in quantity. The only combat aircraft of American design to be developed during the war was the twin-engined Martin bomber, powered by two Liberty engines, but this was not completed in time to see war service.

The Liberty engine represented the most outstanding wartime development of the American industry, and was used both by America and the Allies, some 16,000 being built before the end of the war. The only other quantity-built engine of American design was the Curtiss OX-5, some 8,000 of these being used to power training aircraft and, in addition, nearly 8,000 Hispano-Suiza and Le Rhone engines were built under licence.

Despite tremendous efforts, however, the final balance of American-built aircraft in the Zone of Advance on November 11, 1918, showed clearly how the industry had failed through lack of foresight. Out of a total of 1,005 machines, only 325 DH4s were American-built; of 740 aircraft in squadrons, only 196 were DH4s.

But if the supply of machines had been disappointing, it was reasonable to assume that the lean-limbed, keen-eyed Americans who were to fly them, progeny of adventurous forbears, would be equal to the challenge: and they were, in full measure. Their task required courage of a high order, for it was no sinecure for inexperienced aircrew to be flung into combat against an enemy that had been hardened and sharpened by three years of war. No doubt their fighting spirit was aroused by the exploits of aces like Fonck, Guynemer and Nungesser of France, Ball and Mannock of Britain and Bishop of near-at-home Canada. Less elevating were the achievements of the German aces, Boelcke, Immelmann and the famous Baron Manfred von Richthofen.

From the outset it was clear that a tremendous number of flying personnel were necessary. Unfortunately, there was a complete ignorance of what was needed to train a pilot for combat conditions in Europe. Few, if any, Aviation Section pilots had flown in a combat aircraft: none had ever been engaged in combat.

Realising that this knowledge could come only from the Allies, the Aviation Section wisely decided to concentrate on ground and primary flying training at home, and for advanced flying training to be given in Europe, where experienced instructors would be available. Initiation of a ground training scheme was fairly easy, but provision of primary flying training was a more difficult task because, in the main, the flying schools with their aerodrome facilities had to be built first. Canada provided interim facilities during the summer of 1917, until the Americans could get their schools under way, and eventually there was a total of 27 fields in the US, mostly in the southern states, where almost-all-the-year-round flying was possible.

Fortunately, there was no serious problem in providing a suitable training aircraft, for the Curtiss JN ("Jenny") series was not only built in very large numbers, it proved also to be a valuable and reliable trainer, comparing favourably with the equally well-known Avro 504 of the British air service. Major production centred on the JN-4D—of which over 4,000 were built—powered by a 90 hp Curtiss OX-5 engine, and distinguished by large cut-outs in the trailing-edges of the upper and lower wing, to improve visibility for the occupant of the front cockpit.

Advanced flying training in Europe was handicapped not only by lack of facilities, it had also to take second place to the more urgent needs of the Allies. As cadets began to stream into France, they found themselves waiting for months before they could complete their training, during which period they suffered the standard service cure-all for boredom—drill, cook-house fatigues, spit-and-polish and, of course, guard duties. The cadets at Issoudun, who received the then-enormous pay of $100 per month, became known as the " Million Dollar Guard". It was not until August 1917 that the American Expeditionary Force (AEF) began construction of its own flying schools in France: by late 1918 they were sufficiently established and experienced to give final training to some 2,000 pilots a month.

Unfortunately, air forces require more than pilots to keep their aircraft in the air: they need, too, a whole host of specially trained men to cope with the complex engineering and logistical requirements that add up to an efficient combat force. Schools for specialist officers were established quickly and thousands completed courses during 1917–18. It had been hoped that mechanics in sufficient quantity would be culled from civilian sources, but hopes were dispelled quickly as a growing demand from all industries made them more precious than gold-dust. Again, training schools were needed to solve the problem, and somehow the need was met—more than 10,000 men had completed their courses by May 1918. With pilots and aircraft, and ground crews to keep them flying, it was at last possible to go to war.

At the outbreak of war there had been five US Army aviation officers in Europe: included in their number was Maj. William Mitchell, air observer in Spain, who lost no time in obtaining permission to visit the front. He managed to spend ten days there and, on his own initiative and with French assistance, drafted a plan for an American air force in France. By the time General Pershing arrived with the staff of the AEF in June 1917, Mitchell was the best-informed officer of the Aviation Service.

He proposed to Pershing an Air Service of two components, the first to comprise squadrons specifically for Army co-operation, under the control of ground commanders; the second to consist of "large aeronautical groups for strategical operations against enemy aircraft and enemy material, at a distance from the actual line . . . (which) . . . would have an independent mission . . . and would be used to carry the war well into the enemy's country".

In making these proposals, Mitchell showed that he was one of the pioneers of the concept of strategic bombardment and unified air command, later advocated by Maj. Gen. Hugh M. Trenchard, architect of British air power. At no time in World War I, however, was permission granted to establish an American strategic bombardment force. In fact, the composition and rôle of the Air Service in France was dictated largely by the aircraft available to them, comprising in the main machines which the Allies could spare from their own urgent requirements, for by the time that America was able to turn out the aircraft she needed the war was over.

But in 1917, AEF headquarters in Paris had no 'planes at all. Their first concern was to create a staff and command organisation able to cope with its Air Service when it materialised. Brig. Gen. William M. Kenly was appointed Chief of Air Services, AEF, with Bolling as Assistant Chief in charge of supply, and Mitchell became Air Commander, Zone of Advance. In November, Brig. Gen. Foulois arrived in France and immediately took over from Kenly as Chief of the Air Service.

The growing pains were still hurting: by spring 1918, lack of progress caused Pershing to bring in Brig. Gen. Mason M. Patrick as Chief of Air Service. Foulois became Chief of Air Service, First Army, with Mitchell as subordinate. When, in October 1918, Mitchell was promoted to Brigadier General and appointed Chief of Air Staff, Army Group, he had achieved his ambition to become America's outstanding air combat commander.

There were, of course, Americans who had felt strongly enough about the war in Europe to turn a blind eye to their country's policy of isolation. From 1915 American volunteers had been flying in the British and French air forces and had gained a reputation for skill and courage. Those who chose to fight with the French had first to overcome the problem of nationality, and this was achieved by joining the Foreign Legion. One of the earliest recruits was the colourful, French-born, Raoul Lufbery who, on May 24, 1916, joined the Escadrille Lafayette—a unit composed entirely of American pilots. He scored his first victory against the enemy on July 30, and in October won his fifth victory and recognition as an ace. Within a few months he had brought his total number of victories to 17, ranking him third in the final list of American aces.

It was the Escadrille Lafayette which, in February 1918, formed the nucleus of the 103rd Pursuit Squadron, first American squadron to fly as a unit in action. The 1st Aero Squadron, last heard of at Columbus, New Mexico, arrived in France on September 3, 1917, and were the first American flying unit to reach Europe.

More squadrons arrived before the end of the year, and at the beginning of 1918, in February and March, the 94th and 95th Pursuit Squadrons arrived in the Zone of Advance. Unfortunately, the Nieuport fighters that equipped these squadrons were without machine-guns. When this trifling omission was appreciated and rectified, it was discovered that the pilots of the 95th Squadron had received no gunnery instruction. This gave to "94", the famous "Hat-in-the-Ring" Squadron, the honour of being the first American squadron to go into combat, on April 3, 1918. Eleven days later, Lts. Alan F. Winslow and Douglas Campbell scored the first victories when they destroyed two German aircraft.

Among the pilots of this squadron was a man who had already made a name for himself on the motor racing tracks of America, Lt. Edward V. Rickenbacker. He scored his first victory on April 29, and by the end of May had brought his total to five, ranking him as an ace. His final score of victories might have been considerably higher, but a mastoid operation and convalescence occupied June, July and August, and it was not until towards the end of September that Rickenbacker—newly promoted to Captain and in command of the squadron—began to add to his score. During the month of October he destroyed no fewer than fourteen enemy aircraft, and ended the war as America's top-ranking ace with a total of 26 victories.

Close on his heels came 2nd Lt. Frank Luke, nicknamed the "Balloon Buster", who in a meteoric seventeen days of spectacular aerial combat scored seventeen victories. He had come to the 27th Aero Squadron, 1st Pursuit Group, based at Saints, via the "Million Dollar Guard" route. His most brilliant exploit came on September 18, 1918. While on patrol he spotted two balloons over Labueville. Signalling his team mate, Lt. Wehner, to protect him from the rear, he pulled his aircraft over into a steep dive and destroyed both balloons. As he climbed away he saw that Wehner was being attacked by a flight of six Fokkers; he immediately joined the fray and shot two of them out of the sky. Losing sight of Wehner, and believing that he had made good his escape, he headed for home. *En route*, he found himself in a good position to attack an enemy Halberstadt two-seater. A well-placed burst of fire sent it spinning down in flames, giving him a total score of two balloons and three aircraft destroyed in ten minutes! Elation at his victories turned to bitter regret when he later discovered that Wehner, shot down by one of the Fokkers, had sacrificed his life to protect him.

There are many people who, either from ignorance or prejudice, believe that America's contribution to war in the air came too late to be of any real value. Others think that the sum total of her efforts were confined to the achievements of individuals like Rickenbacker, Luke and Lufbery, men whose names are remembered by countless numbers on both sides of the Atlantic, while those of the senior officers who prosecuted the war are known only to historians.

Both views are wrong. The youthful reinforcements with their let's-end-it attitude was just the medicine the Allies needed at that time: their intervention marked the beginning of the end for Germany. Indeed, many people are unaware that one of the outstanding aviation actions of World War I, which came in the closing months, was also the Air Service's greatest exploit.

For nearly four years the Germans had held a salient which penetrated deeply into the French lines at St.-Mihiel. Before a general advance could be made on this front it was essential that the enemy strong-point should be wiped out. To achieve this the Air Service, First Army—commanded by Mitchell—was cleverly concentrated along an eighty-mile front. To carry out the pre-attack reconnaissance flights Mitchell allowed only minimal air activity, seeking to deceive the Germans of his true strength.

There is little doubt that the ruse succeeded for, by September 12, the date assigned for the attack, Mitchell controlled an American and French air force totalling almost 1,500 aircraft ". . . the largest aggregation of air forces that had ever been engaged in one operation on the Western Front at any time during the entire progress of the war".

When the ground forces went forward on September 12, Mitchell spent two agonising days when the weather prevented him from launching his vast fleet against the enemy: it was not until the 14th that he was able to set his plan into action. Almost a third of his aircraft—some 500 observation and pursuit machines—operated in support of the troops on the ground; the remainder struck hard at lines of communication, installations, reinforcement columns and other targets well behind German lines.

Tactical surprise and, for the first time, numerical superiority in the air, enabled Mitchell to maintain the initiative despite heavy losses on both sides. War-weary troops, foot-slogging it through the mud and misery below, were so heartened to see, at long last, an umbrella of their own aircraft, that within days the Allies were advancing everywhere along the line.

Collective and individual achievements such as these show that despite all the difficulties, the American Air Service put up a commendable performance. They scored their victories: they suffered defeats. They killed enemy pilots and they, in turn, met death in a plummeting dive to the mud and blood-stained arena below. Perhaps less of them would have died had they not considered the parachute a mark of cowardice; at the very least it seemed to suggest a lack of confidence in their machines or their own ability. But above all, they learned the bitter cut and thrust of war the hard way. When the Armistice came they claimed 781 aircraft and 73 balloons destroyed, although the true figures were probably less. The real numbers didn't matter anyway. The Air Service had been blooded in war and could, by virtue of its experience and hard-won confidence, expand from strength to strength. With the maelstrom of war in Europe ended, the AEF returned home triumphantly to enjoy a hopeful peace.

They soon discovered that there was nothing especially triumphant about the peace. The wartime machinery of expansion was thrown quickly into reverse: orders for 13,000 aircraft and 20,000 engines were cancelled within days of the Armistice. Demobilisation of the near-on 200,000 men in the Air Service began immediately, and by June 30, 1920, only 10,000 officers and men remained. The aircraft industry, which had grown to a giant during the war, dwindled to almost nothing. For the next decade the Air Service was to exist on aircraft and engines left over from the war.

Most important post-war task was to settle organisation of the Air Service. The Army Reorganization Act of 1920 made the Air Service a combatant arm of the Army with an authorised strength of 1,516 officers, 16,000 other ranks; these to include a maximum of 2,500 cadets. It was also given control of research and development with authority to purchase its own aircraft and related equipment. On matters of research and development it was to be helped and guided by the National Advisory Committee for Aeronautics (NACA), which carried out a rôle comparable with that of the Royal Aircraft Establishment in Great Britain. In the same way, it has since made an immense contribution to the whole science of aviation, and is justly renowned for its extensive research into aerofoil sections. It was this embryo establishment that moved to its new home at Langley Field, Virginia, soon after the war.

There was, however, another post-war problem that was more difficult to resolve. Those officers who had thought deeply concerning the potential of air power were convinced that it would be the dominating factor of any future war. Foremost of the radicals was Mitchell, audacious and outspoken, and it was inevitable that he should champion the causes of strategic bombing and air, rather than naval, defence for the United States, which caused bitter feeling between the two services.

In tests carried out during July 1921, Martin-built NBS-1 (Night Bomber, Short Range) aircraft of the Air Service sank three ex-German warships anchored in Chesapeake Bay. One of their number was the "unsinkable" battleship *Ostfriesland*. They repeated the exercise in 1923, off Cape Hatteras, when two obsolete US battleships, the *Virginia* and *New Jersey* were also sunk.

The Mitchell faction were jubilant at this success: it was conclusive proof that naval craft could be dominated by air power, that the Air Service, and not the Navy, would be the dictators of future strategy.

The Navy, on the other hand, were not slow to point out that the vessels concerned had been stationary hulks, unmanned and unprotected, and that had they been in a position to retaliate or take evasive action, the final analysis might have been very different.

Naval opinion, prestige and power, backed by Congress, outweighed the theories and arguments of Mitchell and the Air Service. The concept of air power for national defence was killed, and joint Army-Navy coastal defence for the United States had to be forged in the heat of another war. So far as the Navy was concerned, however, the tests had not been a complete waste of time and money, for from that time they began to lay the foundations of their own air arm, culminating in the eventual use of aircraft carriers as the major weapon of seapower.

Mitchell was bitterly disappointed at the turn of events, and continued his campaign at any and every opportunity. Impatience and outspoken comment led to his downfall for, after the loss of the Navy dirigible *Shanandoah* in 1925, he issued a statement to the press, accusing high command of the Army and Navy as being guilty of "incompetency, criminal negligence, and almost treasonable administration of the National Defense". The inevitable court-martial, which Mitchell had hoped to use as a platform to make even more public his convictions of the need for a bigger, better and independent air force, found him guilty, and he was suspended from the Air Service.

Many of Mitchell's criticisms of the existing Air Service were completely valid: unfortunately, the War Department was powerless to remedy them. There were, for example, nearly 2,800 aircraft in service or in storage. Most were obsolete and should have been replaced. In the twelve months which ended on June 30, 1921, no fewer than 330 crashes occurred, killing 69 officers and injuring severely 27 others. A force with less than 900 pilots and observers could not countenance peace-time attrition on such a scale.

By July 1, 1924, total strength had fallen to 1,364 aircraft. Of these, only 754 were in commission, comprising 457 observation, 59 bomber, 78 pursuit and eight attack aircraft; the balance were largely trainers. Maj. Gen. Mason M. Patrick, Chief of the Air Service, recommended a force comprising 20 per cent observation and 80 per cent combat aircraft, and it can be seen clearly that this was a far cry from the circumstances that existed, but there were no funds available to redress this imbalance. In 1925 Patrick commented that there was not enough money to "provide aircraft in numbers adequate to equip completely the present tactical units, much less to provide a war reserve". He considered the only possible course was to continue with experiment and research until the most suitable types of aircraft had been developed, then, if war came, these could be built in quantity.

There had already been some experimentation: bomber aircraft which appeared in the 1920s included the Barling bomber, a six-engined—but considerably underpowered—triplane weighing more than 42,000 lb, and the twin-engined Curtiss NBS-4 Condor, which was the first successful 100 mph bomber aircraft. It was, however, the indifferent performance of these machines which influenced the Air Service to concentrate upon the development of pursuit aircraft, a quirk of fate that was to have far-reaching consequences. The pursuit aircraft which, more than any other, was responsible for this decision, was the single-engined Curtiss PW-8 Hawk, which had a top speed of 178 mph and ceiling of 22,000 ft. One other significant type appeared during this period, intended for low-level attack in co-operation with ground troops: the Curtiss A-3 Falcon, which was built in considerable numbers in the late 1920s.

But there was never enough money. Inadequate funds for development, pitifully small appropriations for training. In fact, aviation on a shoestring. It is surprising only that the Air Service achieved so much.

On the training side they managed to create a reserve of 7,000 officers by 1926, with the National Guard as another source of reserve strength. Primary and advanced training were established at Brooks Field and Kelly Field respectively, both at San Antonio, Texas. Chanute Field, Illinois, had technical schools for both officers and men; McCook Field, Ohio, provided engineering training; and the Air Service Tactical School at Langley Field, Virginia, trained promising officers for high rank and taught the tactical employment of military aviation.

There were accomplishments too, the pay-dirt panned from a conglomerate of enthusiasm, curiosity and pride: a pride that wanted to show the nation that its air arm was sufficiently mature and capable of self-command.

These accomplishments included transcontinental flights, like the 2,520-mile, twenty-six-hour-fifty-minute flight of Lts. Oakley G. Kelly and John A. Macready, from New York to San Diego. Altitude and speed records were won; as in 1925 when Lts. Cy Bettis and Jimmy Doolittle won the Pulitzer and Schneider Cup races within a fortnight. Experimental work was carried out as, for example, the pioneering of flight refuelling in 1923. Two months later, Lts. Lowell H. Smith and John P. Richter set up a new world's endurance record of 37 hours 15 minutes using this technique, their DH4 biplane being refuelled from another aircraft of the same type. There were, too, flights to establish civil air routes, mail-carrying flights, transport operations, border patrol duties, as well as crop-spraying and fire-detection.

But the best-known of all these early exploits was an attempted round-the-world flight made by four Douglas World Cruisers—50-ft-span biplanes mounted on floats, each powered by a single 450 hp Liberty engine.

The four aircraft were individually named *Seattle, New Orleans, Boston* and *Chicago*: the first-named aircraft was piloted by Maj. Frederick L. Martin, who was also in command of the flight. After a lengthy period of preparation, the four aircraft struggled off the water just before dawn on April 6, 1924, and climbed away into a hazy sky and high adventure.

The first instalment was not long delayed for, later the same day, Major Martin became blinded by driving snow and side-slipped thirty feet into near-freezing sea water. Fortunately, damage was limited to broken struts and bracing wires. Five days later, at Sitka, Alaska, the entire expedition almost came to disaster when an unexpected gale swept the *Boston* and *New Orleans* away from their moorings: the situation was saved only by six hours of exhausting work with mooring ropes in water that was colder than charity.

Catastrophe and an adventure that almost ended in tragedy came on April 30, when Major Martin and his companion, Sgt. Harvey, who had been forced down by engine trouble at Chignik, attempted to catch up with the other three aircraft at Dutch Harbor in the Aleutian Islands. Shortly after take-off fog closed in around them; a nightmare experience as they were surrounded by mountains. In his book, *Heroes of the Air*, Chelsea Fraser records the words of Martin, who: "Thinking to get above the fog, where visibility ought to be much better, I pointed the plane's nose upward. We had been climbing for several minutes when suddenly another mountain loomed up ahead. I caught a glimpse of several dark patches—bare spots where the snow had been blown off the jagged rocks. These came at me with the speed of an express train— straight into my very face! Involuntarily I flinched and winked. As I did so there came above the roar of our engine, a sickening, splintering crash. A violent jar accompanied it, and Harvey and I were almost pitched headlong out of our respective cockpits."

The *Seattle* was a wreck, but by great good fortune neither Martin nor Harvey was seriously hurt. The most serious problem was to find their way back to civilisation, on foot. It was not until May 5 that the two hungry, near-exhausted and snow-blind men stumbled on an empty log cabin inside which, miraculously, they found a cache of food and a small wood-burning stove. It was their salvation: heavy snow storms raged for the next two days, and without this shelter they would have died. Eventually, on May 10, they limped into Port Moller and radio soon informed the world that Martin and Harvey were safe.

The full story of the flight is one of excitement and endeavour, unfortunately too long to be recounted here. Suffice it to say that the *Boston* sank under tow near the Faroes, but that the *Chicago* and *New Orleans* triumphantly concluded the 26,345-mile flight at Seattle on September 28, 1924.

As well as the headline-making events, there was the far larger volume of day-to-day, routine, and often infinitely boring activities that served through enthusiasm and sheer hard work to improve the standard of American aviation generally—and of its equipment—both for peace and war.

But the time had not yet come for the Air Service to become independent, though in the mid-twenties the cause had its champions, including the Lassiter Board, who were in favour of bombardment and pursuit groups to carry out independent missions in time of war, under command of the Army. There was, too, the Lampert Committee of the House of Representatives who, in 1925, proposed a unified air force, independent of either Army or Navy.

There was also another Board, headed by Dwight W. Morrow, appointed by President Coolidge in September 1925. The Morrow Board rejected the idea of an independent air force, but recommended that the Air Service should be renamed the Air Corps, to give added prestige. The findings of this Board were accepted by Congress and on July 2, 1926, the Air Service became known as the United States Army Air Corps.

The Act made other changes too, but did not alter the position of the air arm within the War Department, which remained essentially the same as before. There was, however, one shaft of pure sunlight to lighten the prospect: the Act gave authorisation for a five-year expansion programme. Now there was to be some money: perhaps, at last, the Air Corps would find itself in a position to "pursue a different course".

Great Problems

Our first ideal is our country, and we see her in the future, as in the past, giving service to all her people and to the world. . . . She has great problems of her own to solve, very grim and perilous problems. . . .
Henry Cabot Lodge. Speech on the League of Nations. 1919

THOUGH PENNED in a different context, Henry Cabot Lodge's words of 1919 are particularly appropriate to the period which embraces this third decade of the history of the United States Air Force. There were, indeed, grim and perilous problems to be solved. True, they were national and international, rather than specific to the air arm of the US, but they had a profound effect on its development during this period.

In the late 1920s America appeared to be riding the crest of a wave of prosperity. There had been a striking recovery from the immediate post-war stringencies and crises, and Republican President Hoover commented: "We in America today are nearer the final triumph over poverty than ever before in the history of any land."

During the war the people of America, many of whom had never owned a company share, patriotically invested in Liberty Bonds, and became conversant with bankers and brokers. When, in the eighteen months leading to mid-1929, stock prices were rising continually, the nation took to gambling. The prospect of making a fortune by the mere stroke of a pen, or a telephoned instruction, was infinitely more appealing than an existence based upon exhausting physical work.

On the surface, it seemed that prosperity had no limits. In fact, it was a pipe dream fraught with danger, and it seems astounding that the so-called economic experts were unable to read the signs more accurately. Even as late as September 1929 their opinion suggested that the country's economy was fundamentally sound.

On October 23 a spate of selling commenced and Wall Street was soon overwhelmed. The following day—long remembered as Black Thursday —came panic and collapse. Worldwide depression followed quickly. Banks closed their doors, currencies failed, factories stood empty and silent. Everywhere there was widespread unemployment.

In America the misery spread rapidly, as hundreds of thousands wandered aimlessly about the country searching for work—of any kind.

In the cities, skyscrapers assumed a new and grim rôle as speculators ended their lives in a leap from upper-floor windows. The story goes that hotel receptionists would ask: "You want a room—for sleeping or jumping?"

During the three long and dreary years that followed the situation got progressively worse. It was not until March 4, 1933, when newly elected President Franklin Delano Roosevelt gave his inaugural address, that hope was restored.

The new baby—the United States Army Air Corps—had been born at a difficult moment. The proud parents, after the first rejoicings, discovered—like so many others—that their troubles had only just begun. The old three M's—money, machines and men—still featured large, and there were new and difficult problems. But this is anticipating events somewhat, for the first years of the decade started fairly well.

The five-year expansion programme, authorised in 1926, was delayed by lack of funds, and it was not until July 1, 1927, that this got under way. The Air Corps certainly needed a "shot-in-the-arm", for prior to this time it had grown to only little more than half of the establishment authorised by the Army Reorganization Act of 1920, with a total of 919 officers and 8,725 other ranks. Its aircraft strength numbered fewer than 1,000, of which only slightly more than 300 could be classed as modern by the standards of the day.

The target of the expansion programme was a force of 1,800 serviceable aircraft, 1,650 officers and 15,000 other ranks, to be attained by steady increments throughout the five years. The Air Corps failed to achieve this by only a small margin, not for want of endeavour, but once again through lack of funds, for cuts in its appropriations over the five years averaged almost 40 per cent. Most of the expansion came during the first three years, for the remainder of the programme was dominated by the depression.

By June 30, 1932—the closing date of the programme—the Air Corps numbered 1,305 officers, 13,400 men and 1,709 aircraft in 45 squadrons, and comparison with the target figures demonstrates clearly the efforts that had been made.

During the early years of this decade, opportunity was taken to place on a sound footing a number of important organisational matters. Late in 1926 the Air Corps Training Center (ACTC) had been established at San Antonio, with primary and advanced flying schools, together with the School of Aviation Medicine. Funds which became available under the expansion programme permitted the creation of a "West Point of the Air", also at San Antonio. Randolph Field, which fulfilled this rôle as well as becoming headquarters of the ACTC, was dedicated on June 20, 1930. Unfortunately, no sooner were the new facilities ready for use than depression economies restricted the planned training programme to a maximum of 150 cadets a year.

Another important re-location concerned the Material Division, which had been sited at Dayton, Ohio, in 1926. In the following year this Division moved into modern buildings at Wright Field, provided with laboratories and test facilities that did much to influence technological progress and from where, in due course, came the engineers and logistic experts that were to prove so vital to the future of the Air Corps.

It was apparent that, in the late 1920s, the air arm was at last sinking its roots deeply into fertile soil. Even more pronounced was the advance in aviation progress during the same period. First of many notable achievements came on June 28, 1927, with a 2,418-mile non-stop flight from Oakland, California, to Honolulu, made by Lts. Lester J. Maitland and Albert F. Hegenberger in a Fokker C-2 monoplane, powered by three 220-hp Wright R-790 radial engines. Not only was it the first successful transpacific flight from America to the Hawaiian Islands, it was also the Air Corps' first attempt to use radio beacon navigation for a trans-oceanic flight. Unfortunately, this test proved inconclusive because the receiver worked only intermittently.

Eighteen months later, the Air Corps was able to add an unofficial world endurance record to its laurels when the *Question Mark*, another three-engined Fokker—of the C-2A series which had increased wing span—remained airborne over Los Angeles for nearly 151 hours between January 1 and 7, 1929. Commanded by Maj. Carl Spaatz, with a crew which included Capt. Ira C. Eaker and Lt. Elwood R. Quesada, the flight was accomplished by using the flight-refuelling technique which the Air Service had pioneered in 1923.

Less than three weeks later, on September 24, Lt. "Jimmy" Doolittle made the first completely blind flight at Mitchell Field, Long Island, with Lt. B. Kelsey carried as check pilot in the front cockpit. The following day banner headlines in the *New York Times* introduced a story which began: "Man's greatest enemy in the air, fog, was conquered yesterday at Mitchell Field when Lt. James H. Doolittle took off, flew over a fifteen-mile course and landed again without seeing the ground or any part of his plane but the illuminated instrument board. The occasion marked the first instance in which a pilot negotiated a complete flight while piloting absolutely blind."

Journalistic enthusiasm banished the menace of fog many years too soon, but they could have trotted out almost any number of their showiest adjectives to describe "Jimmy" Doolittle without in any way exaggerating this truly great character of American aviation.

During the early 1930s, newspaper headlines of the "Doolittle Breaks Record" type appeared with almost monotonous regularity. It was their very frequency that made them so important, for they told the public, as well as airline operators and their financiers, that air travel could be fast, could be precise and, above all, could be safe.

Doolittle tells another, more amusing, story about fog. It seems his ability as a pilot was such that when Curtiss had wanted to sell their new P-1 pursuit aircraft in South America, they had asked the Air Corps to grant him leave of absence to act as demonstrator. On one occasion, *en route* to Rio de Janeiro, he emerged from a dense bank of fog with no idea of his position. Happy to see a railway track below, he followed it to a station, identified by the grandeur of a small wooden hut across which was written the word Mictorio. He was puzzled that this did not appear on his map, and even more puzzled some seven or eight minutes later when a second station bore the same name. In complete amazement he abandoned "Bradshaw" navigation when a third station was also called Mictorio.

When he eventually put down at Rio he grumbled to the officer who met him: "I would have been here sooner but for a place called Mictorio which has three railroad stations." The officer, his face set in the solemnity of an official reception, began to smile. "The name is on every railroad station in our country," he said, "it means 'Men's Room'."

One could digress endlessly to recount the almost fabulous career of "Jimmy" Doolittle, but space demands a return to April 12, 1930, when a new altitude record for combat aircraft in formation was set by 19 machines of the 95th Pursuit Squadron, commanded by Capt. H. M. Elmendorf, which attained a height of 30,000 ft. The first blind solo flight made entirely on instruments, without a check pilot on board, was accomplished by Capt. Hegenberger at Dayton, Ohio, on May 9, 1932, and on September 3 of the same year Major "Jimmy" Doolittle set up a new world speed record, over a 3-km course, in a Granville Gee Bee monoplane, at an average speed of 294 mph.

One of the most significant achievements came during July and August of 1934. The Air Corps had been anxious to test its ability to reinforce or supply a distant base by air, but lack of aircraft with adequate range had enforced a long wait. Then, in June 1934, the Air Corps' most important between-war aircraft was introduced into service. This was the Martin B-10 twin-engined monoplane bomber—more of which is detailed later in the chapter—and no time was lost in carrying out a proving flight.

On July 19 a formation of ten of these aircraft took off from Bolling Field, DC, bound for Fairbanks, Alaska, under the command of Lt. Col. "Hap" Arnold. When, on August 20, they landed back at Seattle, they had not only completed successfully a round trip of 8,290 miles, they had also accomplished a non-stop flight of almost 900 miles from

Juneau, Alaska, to Seattle, on the return journey, much of it over water.

These achievements were modest by today's standards, but important "firsts" in the years when aircraft were beginning to grow their flight feathers. They showed that not only was the Air Corps gaining valuable experience and confidence, but that the United States' aircraft industry was beginning to build aircraft of greater reliability. The combined demands of military and civil aviation had at last led manufacturers to believe that investment of their hard-earned cash in research and development could, and would, pay dividends in the long run.

They began to walk, rather than plod along, utilising new techniques and ideas. For example, they adopted all-metal construction, which had been pioneered in Germany by Hugo Junkers; they began to clean-up their aeroplanes with the introduction of the cantilever monoplane wing, enclosed cockpit and retractable undercarriage. Variable-pitch propellers enabled engines to offer optimum performance both at take-off and in cruising flight; the piston-engine was developed steadily to give increased power output and a gradually improving power/weight ratio; superchargers were designed and introduced to maintain sea-level performance at altitude. Above all, the radial air-cooled engine became renowned for its rugged reliability, contributing particularly to the rapid spread of American civil aviation. However, it could be argued that the very success of these engines was responsible for the fact that at the outbreak of the Second World War the USAAC had only comparatively slow tubby-looking pursuit aircraft. In Great Britain and Germany, fast, streamlined fighter aircraft had been built around high-powered in-line liquid-cooled engines, with their so much smaller frontal area. The Air Corps had a long time to wait until the North American P-51 Mustang, with an in-line liquid-cooled engine, proved to be one of the great fighter aircraft of the war.

The steady improvement in aircraft performance, particularly noticeable during the 1920s and 1930s, was of great significance to the Air Corps. Many of its senior, if radical, officers had great faith in the potential of strategic bombardment, despite the fact that early bomber types had been considered so inferior to pursuit aircraft that their development had seemed doomed. This minority of officers were quick to realise that the availability of reliable and more powerful engines would make it possible for aircraft designers to develop aeroplanes specifically for a bombardment rôle, which would offer greater range and offensive capability.

Some manufacturers were able to forsee such a requirement, even though War Department policy appeared to be contrary, and the Boeing Airplane Company of Seattle were first, in 1930, to propose a twin-engined bomber development of their Model 221 Monomail airliner, subsequently known as the B-9. Produced as a private venture the prototype, designated XB-901, was an all-metal low-wing monoplane, powered by two 575 hp Pratt & Whitney R-1860-13 engines, and featured a retractable undercarriage. It accommodated a crew of four in open cockpits and had a defensive armament of two 0·30-in machine-guns. Its maximum speed of 188 mph, service ceiling of over 20,000 ft, range of 540 miles and offensive load of 2,260 lb of bombs, marked a big leap forward.

It was followed by another private venture, this time from the Glenn L. Martin stable, which proved to be the most important Air Corps bomber aircraft of the between-war years. The prototype, designated XB-907, began its service trials at Wright Field in July 1932. After modification it was redesignated XB-907A, but when this aircraft was bought by the Air Corps it took the designation XB-10, and it is as the B-10 that it is best remembered.

Like the B-9 it was an all-metal twin-engined monoplane with retractable undercarriage, but in its definitive form which appeared in 1934 as the B-10B, it featured also enclosed cockpits, a manually-rotated gun-turret in the nose, provision for a bomb-bay fuel tank for long-range missions and armament comprising three 0·30-in machine-guns and a 2,260 lb bomb load. Its two 775 hp Pratt & Whitney R-1820-33 radial engines gave it a maximum speed of 213 mph, service ceiling in excess of 24,000 ft and range of 1,240 miles.

These two new aircraft appeared to offer a bright future to the Air Corps. For the first time performance of bomber aircraft was comparable with—and in the case of the B-10 better than—that of contemporary pursuit aircraft. It seemed that the heavily armed bomber would be able to hold its own against the fighter; that a predominance of pursuit aircraft might be a liability rather than an asset. What is more, the potential of these new aircraft demolished the main point of argument of the opponents of strategic bombardment.

For those officers who, like General Foulois—Chief of the Air Corps from 1931–35—favoured the concept of a strategic bombardment force, the availability of an aircraft as promising as the B-10 was another ace in their hand. They already held some fairly good cards: the McArthur/Pratt agreement concluded in January 1931 had given the Air Corps responsibility for land-based air defence of the US coastline, and in January 1933 the War Department had stated that the rôle of army aviation would include long-range reconnaissance and operations "to the limit of the radius of action of the airplanes".

This improved climate, allied to the introduction of the B-9 and B-10, enabled the Air Corps to press for the development of an even more potent bomber. A design competition, initiated in 1934, called for a multi-engined aircraft capable of carrying a 2,000-lb bomb load over a minimum range of 1,200 miles at a speed of 200 mph or better. Boeing were the only company to propose a design involving more than two engines, and although it meant a fairly costly private venture, they were encouraged by the prospect of large-scale orders if the Army were satisfied with the performance of the prototype.

Boeing Model 299 was the designation of the prototype which they produced to meet the Army's requirement, a military development of a four-engined civil transport known as the Model 300. Early test flights of the protype were made during July and August 1935, and on August 20 this machine made a nine-hour 2,100-mile non-stop delivery flight to Wright Field for its official tests. This aircraft was destroyed in a take-off accident on October 30, but preliminary tests had been so promising that the Army had no hesitation in ordering a test batch of 13 aircraft under the designation YB-17.

The gamble paid off for this aircraft, which had the registered name "Flying Fortress" to signify what Boeing then considered as heavy defensive armament, became known universally as the B-17. It remained in production for almost eight years, and the demands of war required that no fewer than 12,731 examples were built eventually.

That Boeing had more than met the Army's specification is well illustrated by the B-17E of 1941, which had a maximum speed of 317 mph at 25,000 ft, service ceiling of 36,600 ft, range of 2,000 miles with a 4,000-lb bomb load and defensive armament which comprised twelve 0·50-in and one 0·30-in machine-gun. A maximum bomb load of 17,600 lb could be carried at the expense of operational radius. A far cry, indeed, from the DH4s that had equipped the Air Service in 1918.

But even before the B-17 materialised, the Air Corps had already made known its requirements for an even more advanced aircraft known as Project A, subsequently given the designation XBLR-1. Boeing had started work on this aircraft (Model 294) in 1935, a four-engined bomber spanning 149 ft. Gross weight of this machine, later designated XB-15, was 70,700 lb, and it had a range of 5,000 miles.

In the same year the War Department had approved a contract with the Douglas Aircraft Company for a still bigger bomber, the XBLR-2, subsequently designated XB-19. This 212-ft span monster had a gross weight of 162,000 lb, maximum bomb load of 37,100 lb and maximum range of 7,710 miles.

Prototypes of both of these aircraft flew, but as engine development had failed to keep pace with the aspirations of airframe designers, both had to be put on the shelf when they were found to be underpowered. Nevertheless, time and money spent on them had not been wasted: a great deal had been learnt about the constructional problems associated with large aircraft, and this was invaluable when the time came to develop and produce the Boeing B-29 and Consolidated B-36.

It should not be thought, however, that this preoccupation with heavy bombers had relegated the pursuit aircraft to oblivion. On the contrary, design competitions held in 1935/36 led to development of the Curtiss P-36 and Seversky P-35, the first of the Air Corps' all-metal single-seat monoplane pursuit aircraft to feature a retractable undercarriage and enclosed cockpit.

By far the most important of these two aircraft was the P-36, for with design refinement and replacement of its radial by an in-line engine, it became the P-40 Warhawk, last and most famous of the Curtiss Hawks. It was produced in great numbers during World War II, exceeded only by the P-47 Thunderbolt and P-51 Mustang, and served on almost all battle fronts. Maximum production centred on the P-40N, early models of which had a 1,200 hp Allison V-1710-81 in-line engine. Maximum speed of this version was 378 mph at 10,500 ft, service ceiling 38,000 ft and range 240 miles. Armament comprised six 0·50-in wing-mounted machine-guns, and a single 500 lb bomb could be carried under the fuselage.

But these were the aircraft of the future: if we resume our narrative back in 1934 it is to discover that the Air Corps was on the brink of one of its most disastrous peacetime ventures.

It is necessary, first, to explain that in 1933 a young reporter named Fulton Lewis, attached to a Washington newspaper, had been interested by protests from a number of small airline operators, who claimed they had been summarily refused air mail contracts. The fact was that these small airlines did not fit the pattern of a national airways system envisaged by Postmaster-General Brown. By feeding to Lewis suggestions of alleged collusion, these operators hoped that subsequent enquiry and publicity would even their score.

At the beginning of 1934, James A. Farley, then Postmaster-General, was summoned to the White House where President Roosevelt was still energetically wielding his new broom. Anxious to eliminate any doubtful left-overs from the former administration, he ordered cancellation of all existing air mail contracts. Farley agreed, but recommended that operators should continue to fly the mail at reduced rates until the advent of new legislation. Wanting none of this the President sent for General Foulois to enquire whether the Air Corps could take over the task.

The General said "Yes", for he could not resist what seemed a heaven-sent opportunity—on behalf of the Air Corps—of winning friends and influencing people in the new administration. It proved to be a most unfortunate affirmative. On February 9, 1934, with the President assured of the Air Corps' ability to carry out the task, a telegram was despatched to each of the air mail carriers—it concluded: "it is ordered that the following air mail contract be, and is hereby, annulled effective midnight February 19, 1934."

Foulois had ten days in which to prepare for what he regarded a national emergency: "under conditions simulating war conditions, in order to discover every possible peacetime weakness in organization, equipment and training".

Aware that he could not hope to duplicate the very considerable network built up by the civil airlines, he chose 14 main routes, involving some 13,000 air miles, and allocated 500 men and 148 aircraft to operate the service. He made his plans carefully, appreciating that here was an opportunity for the struggling air arm to show what could be accomplished by air power.

Unfortunately, he could neither foresee, nor control, the weather, which during the early months of 1934 proved to be the worst experienced for many years. Snow, sleet and icy gales alternated with dense fog, and even before the Air Corps took over the mail routes two crashes occurred during familiarisation flights, bringing the first three fatalities. The first fatal accident while carrying mail came on February 22, followed quickly by three more deaths and many more serious crashes.

The President, Congress and public alike, were horrified at the turn of events: while Foulois took every possible measure to restore confidence, the national press revelled in a spate of lurid reporting. In no time morale was at a very low ebb. One pilot, looking back at those grim February days, commented: "We were working with planes at least seven years behind the commercial planes. We were asked to do an air power job with a few old ships that had been built to 'co-operate' with ground troops . . . personnel equipment was so poor that the pilots suffered frozen hands, frozen feet, frozen ears. . . ."

Storms and fatalities continued arm-in-arm and on March 10 Foulois was ordered to suspend operations for ten days to give time for some reorganisation. Then, two days before the mail flights were due to be resumed, another fatality in training brought public reaction to a peak, resulting in the appointment of a committee, headed by Newton D. Baker, to study all aspects of military aviation.

But the Air Corps was still saddled with its thankless task. During April newspaper cartoons depicted the President and Farley leading a death march composed of the skeletons of Army pilots. As April gave way to May, growing public anger left little doubt in the President's mind that he would have done well to accept the advice which Farley had proffered at the beginning of February. Without further delay he asked the civil operators to resume mail flights on a temporary basis, until new contracts could be drawn up.

Released from their disastrous operation the Air Corps breathed a sigh of relief: during their three months of responsibility for the mail service they had carried 777,389 lb of mail in almost 13,000 flying hours over 1,590,155 route miles.

Tragic though the operation had been in terms of lives thrown away, it proved to be a blessing in disguise for it pinpointed, as nothing else could have done, the inadequacy of the Air Corps, and the obsolescence of its equipment. It suggested, too, that its training programme and procurement of aircraft had failed to provide a force capable of defending the nation against attack—unless it happened to be a fine day!

Little wonder then that the Baker Board, which made known their observations and recommendations in July, had little faith in the potential of the aeroplane for defence. In their report they had commented that: ". . . the limitations of the airplane show that the idea that aviation, acting alone, can control the sea lanes, or defend the coast, or produce decisive results . . . are visionary, as is the idea that a very large and independent air force is necessary to defend our country against air attack."

The members of the Board were unanimous in this opinion, with a single exception—James H. Doolittle—who appended a minority report expressing his belief that the future security of the nation was dependent upon an adequate air force and that he was: ". . . convinced that the required air force can be more rapidly organized, equipped and trained if it is completely separated and developed as an entirely separate arm. . . ."

Perhaps surprisingly, the Baker Board made a single concession to the concept of air power: it recommended that training and supply should continue to be controlled by the Office, Chief of the Air Corps (OCAC), but that a General Headquarters (GHQ) Air Force should be created as the combat element.

To the proponents of air power the GHQ Air Force, which was established on March 1, 1935, represented a first stepping-stone towards autonomy. Brig. Gen. Frank M. Andrews was appointed its commander, and he selected Langley Field, Virginia, as his headquarters. For his staff he nominated officers who were the most ardent advocates of air power; men who believed in building a powerful strategic bombardment force; men who for the past few years had been quietly promoting development of the modern all-metal monoplane bombers.

With the B-17 in prospect, Andrews recommended the formation of an east coast and a west coast bomber group and requested the purchase of fifty B-17s. The General Staff refused, stating that the Douglas B-18s then in service—a twin-engined replacement for the B-10—were adequate for their requirements.

This appears to suggest that the War Department were dubious of the potential of the B-17, or that it had no faith in its new GHQ Air Force. This was quite untrue. The fact was, that once again, there was precious little money left in the kitty.

During the three years prior to 1936 the General Staff had been fairly generous so far as the Air Corps was concerned. The development cost of Project A (the XB-15) alone had exceeded $600,000, representing more than ten per cent of the whole US Army development budget for one year.

Furthermore, following a national policy which stemmed from isolationist beginnings, the Army was able to arm only for defence: explaining the apparent paradox of why the Air Corps needed long-range bombers for defence—it was the only excuse it could offer to get them.

Last, but not least, War Department anxiety to acquire a maximum number of weapons on a minimum budget dictated that the Air Corps should buy greater numbers of small and comparatively cheap twin-engined bombers, rather than a lesser number of the large multi-engined long-range bombers that the more far-sighted members of her air arm knew were necessary.

Three years later, when the German Führer launched his screaming dive-bombers against Poland—a country that had little more than a shield of courage for its defence—the Air Corps' bomber strength included just twenty-three B-17s.

The USAAC had, indeed, many great problems still to face.

A World of Disorder—1

. . . we cannot insure ourselves against the disastrous effects of war and the dangers of involvement. We are adopting such measures as will minimise our risk of involvement, but we cannot have complete protection in a world of disorder in which confidence and security have broken down.
Franklin D. Roosevelt. "Quarantine" Address, October 5, 1937

". . . A WORLD OF disorder in which confidence and security have broken down." It would be difficult to find a mere dozen words able to describe so aptly the sorry state to which the nations of the world had drifted as the 'thirties of the twentieth century drew to a close.

The decline of sanity had started in the Far East, as far back as September 1931, when Japan had occupied Mukden and the zone of the Manchurian railway. By the latter half of the 1930s Europe was in a state of turmoil, for in October 1935 Italy had invaded Abyssinia, Germany had reoccupied the Rhineland in March 1936 and, in the same year, civil war had broken out in Spain.

In March of 1938 Germany swept Austria into her bag of spoils; and in September she received an appeasement gift of the Sudetenland.

The situation became explosive in March 1939, when Germany occupied Czechoslovakia—her "last territorial claim in Europe"—and in the following month Italy invaded Albania. To complete the picture one should record that Japan had, by what she termed an incident, drifted into large-scale war with China. The catastrophe now recorded in history as World War II was but five short months away.

Little wonder then that, in 1937, Franklin D. Roosevelt was making every effort to keep America from becoming involved in the major conflict that seemed inevitable. His "New Deal" was only just beginning to relieve the depression that had almost brought the country to its knees, and at that time the United States was no better fitted to fight a large-scale war than she had been in 1914. Her air force had dwindled to sixth place among world powers in combat aircraft strength—more than disconcerting at a time when events in Spain were beginning to confirm long-held beliefs that air power could well prove to be the key to victory in a future war.

America's proponent of air power, "Billy" Mitchell, had tried—a few months before his death in February 1936—to make Roosevelt appreciate the urgent need for a powerful offensive air force: he had even predicted that Japan would be responsible for America's involvement. Unfortunately, his timing was still too early. World events had yet to demonstrate that isolation was no longer possible in a "world of disorder", if confidence and security were ever again to have any real meaning.

In fact, in 1937/38, it seemed very difficult to convince anyone of the real need for the long-range bombers that the Air Corps had gone to such pains to develop. An "interception" of the Italian liner *Rex*, 725 miles out in the Atlantic, by three B-17s of GHQAF, was intended to demonstrate just how effectively these new aircraft could extend America's perimeter of defence. It succeeded only in sparking off trouble with the US Navy. So much so, in fact, that the Air Corps found itself limited to operational flights of no more than 100 miles off shore.

This was only the first blow to GHQAF. In the spring of 1938 the Secretary of War had ordered the Air Corps to restrict its procurement of bomber aircraft in the 1940 fiscal year to light, medium and attack bombers. Then, in May 1938, the Deputy Chief of Staff, Maj. Gen. Stanley D. Embrick, had summed up the General Staff's views on heavy bombers:

(i) Our national policy contemplates preparation for defence, not aggression.
(ii) Defence of the sea areas, other than within the coastal zone, is a function of the Navy.
(iii) The military superiority of a B-17 over the two or three smaller aircraft that could be procured with the same funds remains to be established.

This cut the ground from beneath the feet of the Air Corps and its GHQAF, for such an outlook eliminated completely the very type of mission for which the long-range bombers had been developed. Brig. Gen. Andrews and his Chief of Staff, Col. Hugh J. Knerr, together with the remainder of GHQAF's staff of air power devotees, were dispersed throughout the Air Corps, an action which seemed to end any hope of a strategic air force.

Happily for the United States, as 1938 neared its end, President Roosevelt seemed suddenly to become aware of the rôle to be played by air power. Perhaps he arrived at this conclusion after considering events in Spain; or he may have been impressed by Germany's *Luftwaffe*-backed power-politics; it is even possible that he recalled some of Billy Mitchell's impassioned appeals. Whatever the reason, Roosevelt told Congress in January 1939 that ". . . our existing (air) forces are so utterly inadequate that they must be immediately strengthened".

Reaction was favourable and prompt, for on April 3 a sum of $300 million was voted to enable the Air Corps to obtain a maximum of 6,000 aircraft. In the event, it proved impossible to programme for so many aircraft, but at least there was the prospect of a balanced force of something over 5,000 machines to be available by June 30, 1941.

Such Presidential and Congressional confidence in the potential of air power meant that the Army must needs review its attitude to, and restrictions upon, the Air Corps. In fact, a step in this direction had been taken already in March 1939, when an Air Board began studying how best to utilise air power for defence. When, in September, Gen. Marshall reviewed their findings, he commented that it established ". . . for the first time a specific mission for the Air Corps".

The new rôle included responsibility for guarding the approaches to the US from the Caribbean and Latin America, as well as acquisition of distant bases to extend even further the Air Corps' radius of action. How ironical it must have seemed to men like Arnold, Andrews and Knerr that these missions required the long-range aircraft that they had been denied—and which were not to be available at the moment of real need.

On September 1, 1939, the day that General Marshall had reviewed the findings of the Air Board, Hitler launched the German *Luftwaffe* and *Wehrmacht* against Poland: two days later France and Great Britain declared war on Germany—the Second World War had begun.

Within the frighteningly short space of sixteen days Polish resistance was at an end. The world witnessed a first copy-book demonstration of a new concept for modern warfare—the *Blitzkrieg*. It consisted, essentially, of tight co-ordination between masses of very mobile armour on the ground, aided and protected by an air force that dominated the air. This combination, backed by parachute troops and an active Fifth Column (which is just another name for traitors—actively helping their own country's enemy), proved adequate to sweep all before it.

For perhaps the first time, events taking place in a remote part of the world caused a severe jolt to American complacency. The President lost no time in initiating changes in the neutrality laws, permitting belligerent nations to buy arms from the US, provided they carried them in their own shipping. Welcome news, indeed, for France and Great Britain.

In the period between the Munich crisis and the outbreak of war, aircraft production in Britain had increased tremendously. Unfortunately, this had not been matched by the French aircraft industry. By the end of 1939 these two Allies had ordered a total of 2,500 aircraft from the United States: within a further three months this number had increased to 8,200.

Orders of this magnitude, added to the requirements of the Air Corps, served to boost American aircraft production to a new high tempo. It seemed that it would be but a matter of time before the European Allies could count on receiving worthwhile reinforcements of aircraft.

Unfortunately for France and Britain, time had already run out. By May 1940 Germany had eliminated Denmark, Norway, Holland and Belgium. In June, France capitulated.

It would be an understatement to say that America was shocked by the fall of France. For the first time since the beginning of World War II, Americans began to question whether distance was any longer protection against the virulent aggression that was spreading so rapidly throughout Europe. There seemed little doubt that the infection would soon spread beyond its present boundaries.

Overnight, national defence became a national concern: and to the nation as a whole the Air Corps seemed to offer the surest means of defence. When General Arnold appeared before Congress in June 1940, he was offered a blank cheque to create an air force of 50,000 Army and Navy aircraft without delay, plus an annual production rate of 50,000 aircraft—a figure which the President had called for a month earlier.

Such a vast quantity of machines, virtually "off-the-shelf", could not have been bought from the American aircraft industry at that time for all the money in the world—neither they nor the productive capacity to build them existed. In an attempt to arrive at more realistic estimates, the War Department asked for 18,000 aircraft by April 1, 1942. But appropriations multiplied quicker than rabbits, to the extent that within twelve months authorisations for Army and Navy aircraft had climbed back to the 50,000 figure again.

It was obviously essential to prepare a long-term assessment of production objectives and the President asked the Secretaries of War and Navy to work out a realistic estimate. On September 11, 1941, their report was made and proved to be a remarkably accurate forecast of the air force's requirements to fight a simultaneous war against Germany and Japan. It called for 239 combat groups, 63,467 aircraft and 2,164,916 men to provide a maximum effort against Germany by 1944. The USAAF's peak strength totalled 243 combat groups, 80,000 aircraft and 2,400,000 men.

There was, of course, a long and difficult road to follow before production could begin to promise even a hint of such figures. Manufacturers, remembering vividly their plight in 1919, required legislative safeguards before committing themselves to such scales of production. Furthermore, entire new factories needed to be built and equipped.

A measure of early achievement is given by a total of 22,077 military aircraft of all types delivered between July 1940 and December 1941: of these, only 9,932 went to the Army's air arm.

No less a problem was the expansion of Air Corps training programmes to provide the necessary men to fly and maintain such a vast fleet of aircraft. By December 1941 improvisation and sheer hard work had achieved some remarkable results, for the number of trained men had risen to 354,000, of which 9,000 were pilots: unfortunately, there were little more than 1,000 first-line aircraft available for them.

This rapid rate of expansion meant, too, that the organisational set-up which had served the between-war requirements of the country and its air arm was no longer adequate: in the year prior to December 1941 very considerable changes were made.

Growing concern about the deficiencies of the nation's air defence had brought the first changes in March 1940, when four "numbered" air forces were created. These were the First, Second, Third and Fourth, responsible respectively for the north-west, north-east, south-west and south-east areas of the United States. On April 12, each of these air forces was ordered to create a bomber and an interceptor command: the former was intended for the support of its respective army in the field, the latter to embrace the whole aspect of defence, comprising early warning, anti-aircraft batteries and defence squadrons.

Training became the responsibility of two commands, with Technical Training Command directing the schooling of ground crews and technicians, while Flying Training Command dealt with air crew. The old Materiel Division was split in two, the new section so formed, responsible for supply and maintenance, acquiring initially the title of Air Corps Maintenance Command, changed subsequently to Air Service Command.

Another Command, created in May 1941, had the name Air Corps Ferrying Command (later renamed Air Transport Command), needed originally to ferry American-built aircraft from factory to their trans-atlantic take-off point. A second responsibility of Ferry Command was the creation of an overseas air transport service, and this assumed eventually an importance equal to, if not greater than, the original task. The two main routes initiated by the Command were from Bolling Field across the North Atlantic to Prestwick, Ayrshire via Newfoundland, and from the same base across the South Atlantic to Africa, via Brazil.

In mid-June 1941, Gen. George C. Marshall, Army Chief of Staff, brought about a very significant change in overall command of the air arm. As the pace of Air Corps expansion began to hot up, existing War Department channels became choked with air force business, causing confusion and delays.

Marshall was quick to appreciate that efficiency could be improved immeasurably if the Air Corps could have greater unity and authority. Accordingly, he pushed through Army Regulation 95–5, effective as from June 20, 1941, which created the United States Army Air Force, with Gen. "Hap" Arnold as its Chief. This meant that Arnold, who was also Deputy Chief of Staff for Air, controlled both the Air Corps and the former GHQAF, which by that time was known as Air Force Combat Command.

The enormous expansion of the air arm triggered off by the fall of France was not limited to the home country. With the realisation that isolation no longer guaranteed security, there came a completely new attitude towards the deployment of Air Corps units at bases beyond the national boundaries. In July 1939, for example, only 3,991 Air Corps personnel were stationed outside the US.

The first move came in 1940, when President Roosevelt announced the transfer to Great Britain of 50 reserve destroyers in exchange for extended leases of eight bases on British possessions. Some of these, together with new bases built in Puerto Rico and the Canal Zone, became known as the Caribbean Defence Command, and it is interesting to note that its first Commanding General, Maj. Gen. Frank M. Andrews—in 1939 the "unwanted" commander of the GHQAF—became the first air officer ever to hold a theatre command.

Then, on November 1, 1940, existing air units in Hawaii were organised into the Hawaiian Air Force, under the Hawaiian Department. By December 6, 1941, this Air Force had a total of 237 aircraft, which included 12 B-17Ds. In June 1941, it was decided to garrison the Philippines strongly, and in the following month the Philippine Army was mobilised. General Douglas MacArthur was recalled to active duty to head a new command created on August 4 from the Philippines Department Air Force, and which became known as the Air Force, United States Army Forces in the Far East. Substantial reinforcements of aircraft were rushed to MacArthur so that by December 5, 1941, he had a total of 265 combat aircraft available, which included 35 B-17s and 107 P-40s (Curtiss Warhawk).

Other outlying bases which had AAF squadrons or detachments at the end of 1941 included Gander in Newfoundland, the second in Dutch Guiana, and the third near Anchorage, Alaska; this latter base had just three squadrons of almost-obsolete aircraft.

Considered originally as important bases for North Atlantic defence were those built in Iceland and Greenland, by arrangement with the Danish government. Best-known was the base at Narsarssuak, Greenland, more usually referred to by its code-name of Bluie West 1. Their greatest value came later: not for defence, but as staging posts for immense numbers of comparatively short-range combat aircraft that were flown across the Atlantic to Britain and Europe.

Stocktaking at the beginning of December 1941 showed that the War Department had strengthened its air arm tremendously during the 27 months that Great Britain had been at war with Germany. Total man-power had risen from approximately 26,000 to 354,000, these figures including pilots, which had increased from 2,000 to 9,000, and air mechanics from 2,600 to 59,000. One cause for concern was the fact that there was not a corresponding numerical improvement in the number of first-line aircraft. In 1939 there had been 800, which included a total of 700 Douglas B-18s and Northrop A-17s and just 23 Boeing B-17s.

By December 1941, first-line aircraft totalled 2,486, of which only 1,157 could be classed as modern by the standards of the day. But once again, before criticising the aircraft industry, it should be remembered that it had been busy setting its house in order for large-scale production. Soon, it was to produce vast quantities of aircraft like the Bell P-39 Airacobra, Boeing B-17 Fortress, Consolidated B-24 Liberator, Douglas A-20 Havoc, Lockheed P-38 Lightning, Martin B-26 Marauder, North American B-25 Mitchell and Curtiss P-40 Warhawk, aircraft which, as they became available, were the mainstay of the American Air Force during the early years of the war.

*

In the autumn of 1941 it became increasingly apparent that the Japanese would, sooner or later, take a leaf from Hitler's book. It seemed that the Philippines would be the first choice for an aggressive move, so it was decided to strengthen the AAF in that area. Maj. Gen. Lewis H. Brereton was posted to act as MacArthur's air commander.

His first task was to ensure that the Far East Air Force was ready to meet any attack that Japan might launch against the Philippines. He found formidable problems: uncamouflaged B-17s visible from a distance of 25 miles; inefficient and unreliable communications; two untried radar installations. To pinpoint a single facet of the alarming weakness: there was no oxygen supply for combat aircrews, limiting operational flights to an altitude of about 15,000 feet.

While Brereton was doing his utmost to remedy the situation in the Philippines, the war plans officer of the Pacific Fleet was busy assuring Adm. Husband E. Kimmel, its Commander in Chief, that "never" would Pearl Harbor be attacked from the air.

History has proved the error of this belief, and the story of Japan's surprise attack on Pearl Harbor on Sunday, December 7, 1941, has been told many times and is universally known. Two facets may not be so well appreciated: a Japanese attack upon Australia, or on a British or Dutch possession, might have caused but little reaction in America— Japan's two-hour attack on Pearl Harbor cured the US of isolationism for all time: within those same two hours some 353 Japanese carrier-borne aircraft, launched in two waves some 200 miles north of Oahu, virtually eliminated the US Pacific Fleet.

Seven of eight battleships were either sunk or badly damaged, as were three cruisers, three destroyers and a seaplane tender. A mine-layer and a target ship were also sunk. Of 169 Naval aircraft in Hawaii, 87 were destroyed; of 231 aircraft of the Hawaiian Air Force only 79 remained serviceable. More than 2,000 Americans lost their lives, nearly another 2,000 were injured.

Three days later, the British battleships HMS *Prince of Wales* and HMS *Repulse*, *en route* from Singapore to reinforce the shattered US Pacific Fleet, were sunk by Japanese aircraft.

Thus, within three short days, and by attack from the air, the whole balance of power in the Pacific had passed into Japanese hands.

On December 8, President Roosevelt addressed a joint session of Congress. In a voice deep with emotion he recounted the lightning thrusts of Japan against the Hawaiian Islands, Malaya, Hong Kong, Guam, the Philippines, Wake and Midway Islands. He asked "that the Congress declare that since the unprovoked and dastardly attack by Japan on Sunday, December 7, 1941, a state of war has existed between the United States and the Japanese Empire".

How unhappily had "Billy" Mitchell's beliefs been vindicated. . . .

*

Despite the fact that America had come into the war as a result of Japanese aggression, it had been decided that first priority should be a build-up of military strength to aid Britain in her struggle against the Axis powers in Europe.

Plans were made to amass men, machines and munitions in the United Kingdom in preparation for a landing in France late in 1942 or the spring of 1943. During the period of this build-up, US forces would take no part in ground operations in Europe or Africa, except in emergency.

America's contribution to air power in the European and Middle-East theatres consisted of four air forces, the 8th, 9th, 12th and 15th. First of these into Europe was the 8th, brought into being at Savannah, Georgia, on January 28, 1942.

In February 1942, Brig. Gen. Ira C. Eaker came to England to establish a bomber command headquarters and make preparations to receive his combat units. Commander of the 8th AF, Maj. Gen. Carl Spaatz, arrived in June and set up his headquarters at Bushy Park, near Hampton Court Palace, on June 18. They came with the intention of earning approval, rather than risking to be branded with the World War I appelation of "loud-mouthed Yankees". This was exemplified by Eaker's terse reply to a speech of welcome. His words were simply : " We won't do much talking until we've done more fighting. We hope that when we leave you'll be glad we came. Thank you." It went down well and did much to foster good relations with their British opposite numbers, who had already fought a long and hard battle, learning much in the process. Above all, the Royal Air Force had learnt, the hard way, that large concentrations of heavy bombers were sitting ducks for German fighters if sent on long-range daylight operations without adequate fighter cover.

The AAF, on the other hand, was convinced that its B-17s carried sufficient armament to provide an adequate defensive shield to permit precision bombing in daylight. It remained to be seen whether experience or theory would prove right.

And so, during the early days of August, the 8th Air Force and the RAF worked out plans for a co-ordinated offensive in which they would be responsible for day and night operations respectively, thus mounting a round-the-clock attack on the common enemy.

General Eaker led the first American heavy-bomber operation from Britain on August 17, 1942, when 12 B-17s attacked marshalling yards at Rouen-Sotteville in France, while six other heavies made a diversionary sweep. Strongly escorted by RAF Spitfires they made a successful attack, all the B-17s returning safely to their bases, although some of the fighter escort were lost. Similar short-range attacks, with RAF fighter escort, were made by the 8th AF during the three weeks that followed: in a total of eleven operations only two B-17s were lost. There was understandable elation in the American camp; it seemed their chosen rôle of precision daylight bombing with the "heavily-defended" Flying Fortress would quickly turn the tide of war in favour of the Allies. They were misled by fine weather—which enabled them to achieve better than average bombing accuracy—and a cautious appraisal of these new bombers by the *Luftwaffe*. The American had yet to learn that long-range penetration of enemy air space without adequate fighter escort was an entirely different kettle of fish.

The 8th AF was delayed in acquiring this knowledge by two factors. First of these was due to an urgent appeal from Winston Churchill for assistance in the Middle East. It was decided that initial reinforcements would be sent from India, with Gen. Brereton in command. He arrived in Cairo on June 28 and initiated the US Army Middle East Air Force which, in November, became the US 9th Air Force. With priority over the 8th AF for men and machines, they made an important contribution to the campaign in the western desert. By concentrating on strategic targets in Southern Europe, as well as by attacking enemy ports and convoys, they denied to Rommel's Afrika Korps large numbers of reinforcements and immense quantities of supplies.

Second of the circumstances which delayed the 8th AF from making heavy attacks on the German homeland, was the decision to mount an Allied invasion of North Africa—"Operation Torch". First major amphibious operation in the European theatre, American troops made landings on the French North African coast in the early hours of November 8, 1942, supported by British naval and air forces.

Success of this operation meant that Axis forces in North Africa were faced with having to defend two fronts. As the jaws of the vice closed relentlessly on them they were penned with their backs to the Mediterranean—and air power meant there was to be no "Dunkirk" for the Germans and Italians. More than a quarter of a million troops were forced to surrender to the Allies.

It meant, too, that the Northwest African Air Forces (NAAF), headed by Maj. Gen. Carl Spaatz, could begin to strike at what Winston Churchill termed "the soft under-belly of Europe". It was not to prove all that soft: but the moment had arrived when Allied production was able to provide ever-increasing quantities of war materials.

The Italian island of Pantelleria was first to fall—to air power alone. After NAAF had battered the defenders with more than 6,000 tons of bombs, the garrison surrendered before assault troops reached the island. Air bombardment and invasion of Sicily and Italy were to follow, and it was from North Africa, during the height of the Sicilian campaign, that heavy bombers of the 9th AF carried out one of the USAAFs outstanding air operations in the European theatre of war: a low-level B-24 attack on the Romanian oil refineries at Ploesti.

It had been estimated that almost two-thirds of Germany's crude oil supplies came from the Ploesti fields: a successful attack on this source would not only deprive the Germans of a vital commodity but would, at the same time, render immediate assistance to the USSR. The Russians themselves had made limited raids on Ploesti in 1941 and 1942, and the USAAF had also made an unsuccessful attack on this target in 1942.

Col. Jacob E. Smart, a member of Gen. Arnold's advisory council, originated the plan for a low-level mass attack from Libya. Gen. Brereton, as commander of the 9th AF, was in charge of the operation, and his planning staff decided to attack a limited number of key installations in each of Ploesti's nine major refineries. The general layout of the target complex was known but there was no knowledge of the extent to which the defences had been developed since the 1942 attacks. In order to achieve maximum surprise it was intended to approach the target at low level from the north-west, individual units attacking specifically assigned targets.

A total of 177 B-24s were allocated to carry 311 tons of demolition bombs, 290 boxes of British and 140 clusters of American incendiaries. Each aircraft was provided with a new low-level bombsight and two auxiliary bomb-bay fuel tanks, bringing total fuel capacity to 3,100 gallons.

A flat reproduction of the Ploesti complex was laid out in the Libyan desert and attacked again and again until all the crews involved were familiar with their individual targets. Finally, on July 28 and 29, the entire task force made two co-ordinated attacks on the dummy Ploesti —the second "eliminated" it in just two minutes. Planning and preparation were considered to be as complete as possible.

Soon after dawn on August 1, 1943, the 177 Liberators, in five groups, carrying 1,725 Americans and one Englishman, took off under the command of Brig. Gen. Uzal C. Gent. The first casualties came minutes later when an engine failure caused one of the bombers to make an emergency landing: it crashed, burst into flames, and all but two of the crew were killed. It was also the first of a string of individual events that was to make Ploesti the USAAF's most costly target to date.

All seemed to be going well, however, as the bombers streamed out across the Mediterranean. Approaching Corfu at some 4,000 feet, the formation started a planned climb to 10,000 feet when, suddenly, the leading aircraft banked steeply and dived into the sea. It carried with it the route navigator for the operation. Another aircraft pulled out of formation to make a low-level search for survivors: still heavily laden with fuel and bombs, its pilot found he could not climb back into formation. He turned back across the Mediterranean and set course for base —carrying with it the deputy route navigator.

The events at Corfu caused the five groups to become split into two formations, one consisting of the 93rd and 376th groups, the others numbers 44, 98 and 389. Towering cloud formations near the Albanian border prevented unification of the formation, and soon after 11 am the 376th and 93rd groups reached Pitesti, Romania. Here they changed course to their final turning point at Floresti, coming down to thunder along some 500 feet above the ground. A turn of roughly 50 degrees to starboard at Floresti would align them with a railway track leading directly to Ploesti. Unfortunately, at Targoviste, about half-way along the leg, there was also a railway line some 50 degrees to starboard and the 376th group turned here, followed by the 93rd. It lead directly to the capital, Bucharest, and immediately all Romanian defences were alerted. The element of surprise at Ploesti had gone.

Realising their error, the two groups turned to attack their assigned targets at Ploesti, but they were now approaching them from the wrong direction which made identification almost impossible. They found, too, that the defences were much stronger than estimated, and met a devastating barrage of fire from machine-guns, cannon and heavy anti-aircraft batteries: to add to the confusion dense smoke screens hid targets, factory chimneys and balloon cables alike.

Detailed planning turned to chaos as errors mounted. The official history of the USAAF in World War II describes how:

". . . the 98th and 44th (groups) commanded by Cols. John R. Kane and Leon W. Johnson, arrived at the correct Initial Point just after the 93rd had finished its run. They found the defences thoroughly alerted. Equally bad, they had to fly through fires and the explosions of delayed action bombs left by the 93rd. The two groups would have been justified in turning back; instead, they drove straight against their targets, through intense flak, explosions, flames and dense black smoke which concealed balloon cables and towering chimneys. B-24s went down like ninepins, but their targets were hit hard and accurately. As the two groups left Ploesti they were jumped by enemy fighters, and on the way home were attacked by every kind of plane from Me 109's to unidentified biplanes, the last attacks coming after the Liberators were over the Adriatic."

Final analysis of the Ploesti operation showed results far short of expectations: 54 aircraft and 532 aircrew were lost. On the credit side an estimated 42 per cent of Ploesti's refining capacity was destroyed and perhaps 40 per cent of the cracking capacity was put out of action for four to six months.

The Germans were not slow, however, to reactivate idle units at Ploesti, and this action coupled with repairs to lightly damaged plant soon restored much of the refining capacity. It was not until the following year, between April 5 and August 19, 1944, that heavy bombers dropped some 12,890 tons of bombs on Ploesti in 5,287 sorties, reducing output by an estimated 62 per cent.

While these events had been taking place from the North African theatre the 8th Air Force, based in Britain, had continued to pursue its daylight bombing offensive in Europe. It had proved a painfully slow business to build up the necessary strength to mount a worthwhile attack. The North African campaign had priority for men and machines, which meant that bombers and their crews arrived in England on such a meagre basis that it was not until April 17, 1943, it had become possible to put as many as 100 aircraft over enemy targets in a single day.

In this period it had become abundantly clear that adequate fighter escort was essential if losses were to be contained within acceptable limits. This, in turn, meant that the range of the bombing offensive was governed by the effective range of the escorting fighters. Thus, for about six months from the first B-17 operation, targets had been confined in the main to the Pas de Calais coastline of Northern France and inland as far as Lille, the Atlantic coast from Brest southward and German installations in the area of Rotterdam.

This was the situation in May 1943, when Republic P-47 Thunderbolts began to arrive in sufficient numbers to relieve the Royal Air Force Spitfires which, until then, had shouldered the task of protecting the American bombers. It was a disappointment to the 8th Air Force to discover that, initially, the P-47s offered no improvement in combat range.

During the month which followed a combination of modification and pilot experience brought a slight increase in range, but it was not until August that the addition of a jettisonable belly fuel tank enabled the Thunderbolts to range as far afield as Hamburg. The provision of still more external fuel gave these fighters a tactical radius of about 425 miles and this, at last, enabled the Fortresses to operate in concert with RAF Bomber Command on a round-the-clock basis.

It was a fortuitous moment, for it coincided with the start of Bomber Command's intensive area bombing of large industrial centres—attacks which were concentrated in time as well as area, so that enemy defences became saturated.

So effective was this combination of the USAAF by day and the RAF by night that, by the spring of 1944, 26,000 acres in the heart of 43 German cities had been left in smouldering ruins.

Also in the spring of 1944 the 8th Air Force was reinforced in no small measure when it began to receive steadily increasing numbers of the North American P-51 Mustang, a machine which must be classed as one of the great fighter aircraft of World War II. Produced to meet a British requirement for a fighter—a design which sought to benefit from the lessons of early combat action in Europe—the prototype was constructed in less than four months and flew for the first time in October 1940.

By the time the 8th Air Force received the Mustang this exceptional aircraft had a maximum escort range approaching 1,000 miles, which meant that the fighters were no longer tied closely to the apron strings of the B-17s and B-24s, but could range the skies above and around their charges. The previous over-ruling order to only "protect the bombers" was now extended to "and pursue and destroy the enemy".

The 8th Air Force needed no encouragement and from then until D-Day concentrated on the destruction of aircraft component and assembly plants, ball-bearing factories, strategic rail centres and enemy airfields, ranging out over vast areas of the German homeland and not, of course, forgetting enemy aircraft both in the air and on the ground.

By D-Day the 8th Air Force was in full flood, a potent and proud air force. It had every right to feel that way for it had proved to a sceptical world that daylight precision bombing was a valid concept. It had proved that even individual factories could be hit accurately by day and that because of such accuracy a smaller force would suffice for many targets. It had proved that by maintaining a daylight offensive in concert with the night offensive of the RAF, enemy defences, production units and civilians were kept in a constant state of tension—24 hours a day— with resulting effects on morale and production.

It had proved all these things—but at what a cost. Until the advent of the Mustang the Fortresses, Liberators and their crews had been compelled for much of the time to fight their way to and from their targets. They sought to derive some self-protection by packing about eighteen bombers into a tight formation called a combat box, stacking two or three of these boxes vertically to form a combat wing.

Day after day, in these precise formations, the 8th Air Force shattered the peace of the East Anglian countryside as they set out for their target. Later they would come limping back—on three and even two engines, great gashes in wings and fuselage, often with many of their crews injured or dead.

And the next day, with cold courage bordering on heroism, they did it all over again, and the next day . . . and can you conjure up in the depths of your imagination what it must have felt like when, after losing 60 out of 291 Fortresses sent to attack Schweinfurt, reassorted crews were briefed for the next day. . . .

When Germany surrendered the 8th Air Force had dropped an amazing 701,300 tons of bombs on enemy targets in Europe—by daylight !

Nevertheless, theirs had not been a solitary American battle in Europe, for in September 1943 the 9th Air Force had been transferred from North Africa to Britain with Gen. Brereton in command, until he was replaced by Maj. Gen. Hoyt S. Vandenburg in August 1944. On October 15, 1943, it was reformed as a tactical force composed of fighters and medium and light bomber aircraft, growing rapidly to become the largest single force of its type in the world.

Principal weapons of the 9th Air Force were the P-51 and P-47 fighters, together with the Lockheed P-38 Lightning fighter and the Martin B-26 Marauder bomber, and their first great task was to deny the enemy use of the many large airfields which they had constructed in Belgium, France and Holland. By the end of 1943 they had succeeded to the extent that they could direct their attention to the flying-bomb sites which had mushroomed along the Calais and Normandy coastline.

During the spring of 1944 the force was concerned with pre-invasion activities and their campaign of interdiction was of immense value to the Allies, especially their task during May when they concentrated on bridges over the Seine between Paris and Le Havre.   On D-Day they ranged far and wide in a total of 4,700 sorties, providing fighter cover, escorting troop carriers, carrying out reconnaissance missions, as well as making life tedious for the enemy wherever he was trying to move men and their equipment towards the battle area.

A technique known as carpet-bombing, employed by the 9th Air Force on July 25, 1944, rendered valuable assistance to ground troops held up at St-Lô.   In an area of approximately 7,000 by 250 yards they dropped a total of 3,400 tons of bombs, demoralising the enemy long enough to enable the 1st Army to continue its advance.

Throughout the months that elapsed before the German surrender the 9th Air Force managed, somehow, to be almost everywhere most of the time, by day and night, and the formation of Tactical Air Commands assigned to individual Armies brought valuable assistance to the ground troops, who were able to count upon massive air support of the right type where and when it was most needed.   When, early in 1945, the Germans made a desperate attempt to defend the Ruhr, the 9th had an important part to play in the plan to isolate the area and destroy the transport system within it.

When war in Europe came to an end the 9th Air Force, in a brief period of 19 months, had dropped 239,213 tons of bombs, discharged 74,299,865 rounds of ammunition and blasted the enemy with 13,959 air-to-ground rockets.

But in the end total it was lack of fuel, more than any other single factor, that hastened Germany's collapse.   By day and night the heavy bombers of the USAAF and RAF had pounded enemy manufacturing centres, but despite this miracles of concealment and dispersal had enabled the Germans to maintain enormous stocks of hardware of all kinds, for deployment on land, at sea and in the air.   Without fuel, however, they were all paralysed.

The Western Allies raced eastward—the Russians west—to meet at the River Elbe on April 25, 1945.   Twelve days later Nazi Germany surrendered unconditionally.   Air power had achieved its first major and overwhelming victory.

Statistics give only some measure of achievement in the enormous struggle against the armed might and cruel determination of Hitler's Germany: like so many wartime statistics they are not always reliable and differ from source to source: likewise, they can be interpreted in many different ways.

One figure, however, is cardinal.   Almost 45,000 American airmen of the 8th and 9th Air Forces had, as their contribution to the Allied cause, given their lives in the hope that Europe would forever enjoy the blessings of freedom.

A World of Disorder—2

. . . with confidence in our armed forces—with the unbounding deter-mination of our people—we will gain the inevitable triumph—so help us God.

Franklin D. Roosevelt. December 8, 1941

THE SMOKE and stench of battle still hung around the wreckage of Pearl Harbor as the President spoke these words to Congress. During the previous night men had known fear, felt pain, or lost themselves in death as the Japanese master-plan exploded throughout the Pacific.

And master-plan it was. The aim: to eliminate Allied tenure of an encirclement of bases—pushing them further and further outward—extending the Japanese perimeter of defence which, if policed adequately by her naval and air forces, would effectively prevent the Allies from making an attack upon the home islands.

At only one point did the enemy encounter any serious resistance. A heroic and protracted defence of the Philippine Islands by American and Filipino forces, under the command of Gen. Douglas MacArthur, gave considerable heart to a shattered American nation. It gave also a far greater gift—time for the United States to recover from the initial shock of the enemy's lightning attacks. With a tiny defending force of about 36,000 men, MacArthur tied down nearly 200,000 Japanese troops, their transport and part of the Imperial Navy for four months. He succeeded also in destroying large numbers of men and vast quantities of materials.

MacArthur and his Air Commander, Maj. Gen. Brereton, received early news of the attack on Pearl Harbor. Unfortunately, they had hesitated over the deployment of their aircraft fleet, which comprised 35 Fortresses, 107 P-40 Warhawks, together with some Republic P-35As and a number of obsolete bombers, transports and trainers, totalling in all about 250 machines.

Soon after 8 am on December 8, two squadrons of P-40s were scrambled on reconnaissance patrols, and two squadrons of Fortresses ordered into the air to ensure they were not caught on the ground. Brereton was anxious to use the Fortresses against enemy bases on Formosa, but MacArthur was opposed to this as there had not, at that time, been a formal declaration of war. Eventually Brereton prevailed and, towards the end of the morning, the B-17s began to land back at Clark Field to prepare for the operation. At about the same time, the P-40 squadrons returned to refuel.

Not too many air miles away a mixed force of almost 200 enemy fighters and bombers was *en route* from Formosa. About half of this force attacked the fighter base at Iba Field, which it destroyed completely in a matter of minutes, while the remainder commenced its attack on Clark Field. In about half an hour the base was in ruins, its buildings in flames; all of the precious aircraft were either destroyed or damaged.

This kind of treatment set the pattern for the next two days, by which time Brereton's combat force was reduced to 12 serviceable B-17s, 22 P-40s and eight P-35s. Too few to risk in combat, they were reserved for reconnaissance sorties. Their numbers were reduced steadily in the weeks that followed, but those that could be coaxed into the air continued to provide valuable information until May 7 when, unable to offer further resistance to the Japanese without adequate naval or air support, MacArthur's commander in the field, Maj. Gen. J. M. "Skinny" Wainwright, was forced to surrender to the enemy.

In the six months which followed the attack on Pearl Harbor, Japanese forces swept all before them and, in command of both sea and air routes, were able to expand throughout immense areas of the west Pacific, imposing a grave threat to the security of Australia and India.

The conquest and occupation of this area not only gave Japan the defensive perimeter she had been anxious to possess, but it was also an area rich in natural resources and, as such, an invaluable prize. So long as she could retain command of the sea and air routes that radiated out from the home islands—routes which extended over a radius of some 4,000 miles through a sector from the north-east to south-west of Tokyo —the new Japanese empire was secure.

The Allies were not slow to appreciate that these extremely long supply lines were the enemy's Achilles heel, and no time was lost in mustering every resource, however meagre, to destroy his shipping and wrest from him mastery of the air.

During the eight months extending from April to December 1942, six events occurred that were destined to lead to Japan's final defeat. Since it is not possible within the confines of this chapter to detail the USAAFs participation in the Pacific War it is, perhaps, more pertinent to examine these factors in some depth.

The first two of these events had already taken place before Maj. Gen. Wainwright had been forced to surrender his troops to the Japanese at Corregidor.

During the afternoon of April 4, 1942, a Catalina flying-boat on routine patrol off Ceylon, piloted by Sqdn. Ldr. L. J. Birchall, RAF, sighted a large Japanese naval force some 350 miles south-east of Ceylon, and heading towards the island. He reported the sighting immediately, but no subsequent message was received from Birchall and it was assumed that his aircraft had been destroyed.

Confirmation came at midnight when a second Catalina reported this force, consisting of battleships, cruisers, destroyers and aircraft carriers, to be some 100 miles nearer to Ceylon. Thanks to this advance warning, when Japanese carrier-borne aircraft attacked Colombo harbour and Ratmalana, the British naval base near Trincomalee, the defences were waiting for them.

John W. R. Taylor in a companion volume* comments:

"Almost his (the enemy's) only failure in five months of incredible conquest had occurred further south, where an attempt to emulate the success of Pearl Harbor at the naval base of Trincomalee had been beaten off. Nonetheless, as Admiral Nagumo withdrew eastward in mid-April, he could look back with satisfaction on the fact that his carrier-borne aircraft had sunk 23 merchant ships north of Ceylon, as well as the carrier *Hermes*, cruisers *Dorsetshire* and *Cornwall* and destroyer *Vampire*.

"What he did not know was that, paradoxically, his success helped to ensure Japan's ultimate defeat. He had lost so many aircraft to Ceylon's Hurricanes and Naval Fulmars that three of his carriers had to return to Japan to refit and so were unable to participate in the Battle of the Coral Sea. . . ."

The second event to contribute to Japan's defeat, and perhaps one of the most significant, occurred on April 18, 1942, when sixteen B-25 Mitchell medium bombers made a spectacular low-level attack on the Japanese home island, led by the legendary "Jimmy" Doolittle.

What soon entered the annals of the USAAF as the "Doolittle Raid" originated as early as January 10, 1942, when Capt. Francis Low of the USN made what he considered a rather fantastic proposition to Admiral Ernest King. He suggested, rather diffidently, that he thought it might be possible to convey a small force of Army bombers on board a carrier to within striking distance of the Japanese homeland. A successful attack would do much for American morale—then at its lowest ebb—and simultaneously give the Japanese a severe jolt.

Somewhat to Low's surprise, the Admiral considered the suggestion worth investigation and detailed Capt. Donald Duncan, USN, one of his staff officers and an experienced pilot, to make initial enquiries and report whether or not the idea was practical.

Although a naval pilot, Duncan was reasonably familiar with the

* Pictorial History of the RAF, Volume II.

performance of most Army aircraft; he eventually came to the conclusion that the North American B-25 medium bomber—coincidentally and most appropriately the aircraft which commemorated the name of "Billy" Mitchell—was the only possible contender for the task. Within five days Duncan produced a detailed plan which he presented to Admiral King.

King then approached "Hap" Arnold, and together they sought and gained the approval and blessing of the President. Arnold, excited by the proposal, agreed to allow Duncan to supervise initial tests to see whether a B-25 could get airborne from a carrier deck. Within hours Duncan was able to tell them that a stripped, lightly-loaded B-25 could take off within 500 feet: not long after he confirmed a successful take-off from a new carrier, USS *Hornet*.

Success for a stripped, lightly-loaded aircraft was one thing: could the same aircraft with crew, bombload and more-than-normal fuel capacity do the same? Since many unorthodox changes would be necessary to ensure a reasonable chance of success, "Hap" Arnold knew that he would require an exceptional man to co-ordinate and lead the operation. He needed to be a skilled aeronautical engineer; he needed, also, above-average ability as a pilot. Last but not least, he must possess the divine spark which singles out a leader of men. He chose Lt. Col. "Jimmy" Doolittle.

Almost quicker than you can say "Doolittle", the bearer of that name had reported to Arnold and was a little staggered to be asked, quite simply, whether the USAAF had an aircraft capable of a 2,000-mile-range operation, carrying a 2,000-lb bombload, and able to take off within 500 feet.

Doolittle needed no crystal ball to foresee that such a requirement spelled a carrier operation: his two-and-two made a Japanese four, and he was filled with enthusiasm for the task. It took him but a short time to reach the same conclusion as Duncan, realising equally quickly that weight reduction and other modifications would be needed to give the necessary load/range capability. It took but little longer, at Wright Field, to satisfy himself that he could get a fully loaded Mitchell off the ground within 500 feet.

Sixteen B-25s were allotted to the task and in the weeks that followed Doolittle had them stripped of their Norden bombsights, ventral gun turrets and liaison radios. Fuel tankage of each aircraft was increased to 1,141 US gallons, a "twenty cent" bombsight—designed especially for the operation by Lt. Ross Greening, an armament specialist—and an auto-pilot was installed in each, as well as two dummy guns, fitted in the tail cone, to discourage any stern attack by enemy fighters.

While the crews—drawn from the 17th Bomb Group and 89th Reconnaissance Squadron, both equipped with Mitchells—learned to lift their machines off the ground within the specified distance, Doolittle busied himself ensuring that the condition of each aircraft was as near perfect as possible.

It had been intended originally that fifteen B-25s would be loaded on board the USS *Hornet*, but Doolittle decided to take an additional aircraft along so that, when the carrier was well clear of the mainland, the Mitchell could take off and return to San Francisco. Since none of the crews had seen a B-25 flown from a carrier, it would give them a measure of confidence to witness a successful take-off.

In the last days of March all was ready, and the sixteen aircraft were loaded at San Francisco. On April 1, less than three months from the birth of Low's idea, the *Hornet* put to sea.

The plan of attack, known to only eight men at that moment, was for the *Hornet*, outwardly an ordinary carrier within an everyday task force, to try and approach within four hundred miles of the Japanese coastline. At that point the B-25s would have adequate range both to find their targets and then fly on to landing fields in China, where they would refuel and then *rendezvous* at Chunking.

The greater the distance from Japan at which the force might be sighted or intercepted, the greater the risk. The possibility of a chance meeting with enemy air or naval patrols as far as 1,500 miles from the coastline would have meant committing the aircraft and their crews to a one-way mission with little hope of survival. When Doolittle briefed his crews on board the *Hornet*, not a single man was unprepared to accept the odds.

With San Francisco some 500 miles astern came the moment for the 16th Mitchell to make its demonstration take-off. Characteristically, Doolittle decided it would have far more value as one of his attacking force: his own take-off would have to serve as object lesson and morale-booster.

Sea-miles astern became greater and greater, the target excitingly closer and closer and then, at 06.30 hours on April 18, came the moment of truth. With the *Hornet* still some 800 miles from the Japanese coast, an enemy patrol ship came within visual contact. Immediately, the cruiser *Northampton* was despatched with orders to attack and destroy the enemy. Whatever the outcome, however, it was tolerably certain that Japanese naval intelligence would have been advised of the position of the American force.

Take-off could be delayed no longer, and aircraft and crews were readied as quickly as possible. In *The Amazing Mr Doolittle*, Quentin Reynolds describes the dramatic moment when just about everything depended upon "Jimmy":

"... With full flaps and engines roaring at full throttle, the plane lunged down the deck in the teeth of the gale. Every other pilot was watching the take-off. If Doolittle couldn't do it, they couldn't. Just as the *Hornet* lifted itself to a level position, Doolittle took off with a hundred feet to spare. He hung the ship almost straight upon its props, levelled off, and came around in a tight circle. He had made it look incredibly easy, and every pilot now felt better. Doolittle completed his turn and watched the number two ship take off. Travis Hoover was the pilot. The *Hornet's* deck came up after its pitch unexpectedly fast, and Hoover's plane had to scramble uphill. It took off and dropped abruptly and Doolittle, watching, tried to pray it up. Just before the wheels were about to hit the water, Hoover managed to lift its nose up. Brick Holstrom's plane, Bob Gray's plane, Davey Jones' plane, Dean Hallmark's plane, Ted Lawson's plane, all took off beautifully. But by now Doolittle was headed for Tokyo. . . ."

The time taken to reach the Japanese coastline passed quickly enough, the crews fully occupied in maintaining a minimum clearance between their aircraft and the waters of the Pacific. Over the coast they kept almost at treetop height until Tokyo was sighted and then climbed steeply to their assigned height of 1,500 feet.

Taken by surprise, the Japanese could raise little opposition and all sixteen aircraft were able to attack their targets. Doolittle, Lt. Hoover and one flight of aircraft made for northern Tokyo; Capt. Jones led his flight over the city centre, while Capt. Edwin York's group attacked the southern side and part of Tokyo Bay. Capt. Charles Greening's targets included Kanegawa, the Yokasuka navy yard and Yokohama. The fifth group, led by Maj. John Helger, was responsible for military installations at Nagoya, Osaka and Kobe.

With the attack behind them, their real problems started. It had been planned that the Chinese would "home" Doolittle's force by radio, and landing flares would pinpoint the designated airfields. By a chapter of accidents there was no guidance of any sort: over strange country in bad weather, fuel tanks down to the last sip, the majority had little alternative but to bale out of their aircraft, while others "ditched" just off the coast.

Of those who trusted to their 'chutes, most landed in unoccupied China and, after many adventures, eventually rejoined their units. Eight were, however, captured by the Japanese: three of them were executed, one died of malnutrition and the other four survived rather more than three years of imprisonment. One aircraft, that of Capt. York, was put down near Vladivostock and its crew interned by the Russians.

What was there to show for all this effort?

As Doolittle examined the wreckage of his aircraft in the light of another day, he was convinced that the whole thing was a failure. If damage to enemy installations and production capacity was the yardstick, he was right!

He was not to know, until some time later, that the attacks made by sixteen very brave crews had achieved much, much more. It was almost certainly responsible for the retention in Japan of four fighter groups whose services would have been invaluable in the south Pacific during crucial months of 1942–43. Furthermore, in an attempt to prevent a repetition, the Japanese scrambled still harder to increase their perimeter of defence and, in so doing, over-extended themselves.

Quite positively—and of immense importance—it proved to the American nation and its armed forces that the Japanese were not invincible. Uncle Sam could, and would, hit back.

Suddenly, the skies seemed a little lighter!

The next two of the six events followed closely upon each other, and though not strictly USAAF affairs, they are of significance to our story.

The remnants of the USAAF 19th Bombardment Group from Clark Field, together with surviving aircraft of other bomber and fighter units based in the Philippines, had retreated south through Java to take a stand on the north coast of Australia, where there was considerable fear of Japanese invasion. This had been heightened after the seizure of Rabaul on January 22, 1942, followed by enemy air raids on Port Moresby.

Immediate steps were taken to strengthen Australian defences—an extremely difficult task for the Allies at that moment in time. American forces first secured the islands that would allow policing of the vital routes to Australia, following which reinforcements of men and machines were moved in to meet the absolute minimum defence requirements.

On February 5, 1942, the odds and ends of USAAF units based there ceased to be known as the Far Eastern Air Force and became, instead, the 5th Air Force under the overall command of Maj. Gen. George C. Kenney. During the two months which followed, strength of the 5th increased gradually and within a short time its aircraft were operating in conjunction with those of the US Navy, primarily on reconnaissance.

Patrolling vast reaches of the Pacific could be a monotonous and demanding task. Crews who had suffered already at the hands of the enemy accepted gladly an opportunity to hit back, however demanding the job. Their wide-awake vigilance soon alerted American intelligence to the fact that Japanese forces were concentrating at Rabaul and that a move southward to capture Port Moresby was imminent.

To counter this threat, Admiral Nimitz hastened to assemble in the Coral Sea as strong a naval force as possible. By May 1, this comprised the carriers USS *Lexington* and *Yorktown*, supported by five cruisers; three days later they were reinforced by a sixth American cruiser, plus two more from the Royal Australian Navy.

The Japanese striking force, due to circumstances mentioned earlier in this chapter, consisted of only two carriers, the *Zuikaku* and *Shokaku*, together with two cruisers, and during the two days which followed both forces were involved in a grim game of hide-and-seek. Then, on May 7, reconnaissance aircraft from the *Yorktown* made contact with an enemy force reported as two carriers and four cruisers. Rear-Admiral Fletcher, commanding *Yorktown*, believed he had located the enemy striking force: in fact, it was a weaker group escorting the invasion transports, and included the light carrier *Shoho*. Fletcher reacted immediately and despatched all available aircraft to attack—within three hours the *Shoho* was destroyed and, deprived of air support, the invasion force withdrew.

By this action Fletcher had disclosed his position to the enemy. At about 11.00 hours on May 8, the aircraft of the opposing naval forces struck almost simultaneously. The *Shokaku* was damaged severely, but able to limp home, the *Zuikaku* unscathed. On the American side the *Yorktown* was slightly damaged, the *Lexington* severely damaged and on fire. Heroic efforts by her crew quelled the fires and patched the worst damage so that she could get under way. About an hour later she was devastated by an internal explosion: uncontrollable fires resulted in her being abandoned, and sunk by an American torpedo.

On balance the honours seemed fairly even; if anything, they favoured the Japanese. Why, then, do naval historians rank this as an important action in the air/sea war in the Pacific?

It was, similarly to the "Doolittle Raid", a psychological victory for the Americans—the first successful naval action against the Japanese. The USN had discovered that the enemy could be beaten at his own game. Furthermore, the invasion force menacing Port Moresby had been forced to withdraw. It was, incidentally, the first ever naval battle fought entirely by carrier-borne aircraft, without the opposing ships firing a single shot at a surface vessel. The concept of air power, demonstrated by the Army when their aircraft had sunk the "unsinkable" *Ostfriesland* in 1921, and its chief proponent, "Billy" Mitchell, were clearly vindicated.

To the Japanese it posed a problem that needed an instant solution, for they could not countenance naval domination of the Pacific by their enemy. At all costs the American fleet must be brought to battle and destroyed.

Admiral Yamamoto's plan was to seize Midway Island, together with its airfield, from which Pearl Harbor could be threatened and, at the same time, attack the western Aleutians. By careful timing he hoped to draw the American fleet from Midway so that he could take this island with little opposition: by the time the USN realised his true intentions he would be in possession of Midway and ready to meet any attack with overwhelming force. Knowing that the island was vital to American strategy it was inevitable that a major naval engagement would follow and, by virtue of his superior strength, especially in fast battleships, Yamamoto felt confident of the outcome.

Admiral Nimitz, however, well primed by intelligence and fully aware of the importance of Midway, made haste to prepare for the coming battle. Though his force was numerically inferior to the enemy he had at least one card up his sleeve: he could count on powerful air support from squadrons of the 7th Air Force on Midway.

On June 4, reconnaissance aircraft of the 7th Air Force reported the position of the Japanese aircraft carriers. Immediately, torpedo-bombers from the USS *Enterprise*, *Hornet* and *Yorktown* pressed home an attack. The enemy's defence was too strong and the attack unsuccessful, but with Japanese fighters concentrating on the destruction of the torpedo-bombers, a force of 37 dive-bombers from the *Enterprise* and *Yorktown* were able, almost unopposed, to attack Admiral Nagumo's flagship, the carrier *Akagi*, and her sister ship the *Kaga* and, almost simultaneously, 17 aircraft from the *Yorktown* pressed home their attack on the carrier *Soryu*. Within minutes, all three ships were ablaze from stem to stern; devastating fires raged below decks and it was quickly apparent that they were doomed.

Fierce retaliation by the Japanese seriously damaged *Yorktown*, and although her fires were got under control, she was attacked again and finally sunk by an enemy submarine two days later. But long before *Yorktown* disappeared below the unrelenting Pacific, the fourth and last of Yamamoto's carriers—the *Hiryu*—had met a flaming and bloody end as men and aircraft from *Enterprise* sought revenge for the loss of their sister carrier. Within hours Yamamoto ordered a general retirement of his forces.

Generally regarded by historians as the turning point of war in the Pacific, there is little doubt that it was a major victory for American air power, shore and ship-based aircraft operating in concert. The Japanese had lost four fleet carriers and a large number of their most highly skilled aircrew. Neither could be replaced. What is more, it was abundantly clear that first-class aerial reconnaissance had played a significant part in the American victory. Even the most ardent advocates of naval power must have realised then, if never before, that the largest battle fleet was at the mercy of an enemy who could dominate the air.

The fifth event had its origins as far back as 1934, when the GHQAF had planned development of long-range bomber aircraft. One of these had been known as Project A and a contract for the construction of one aircraft, under the designation XB-15, had been issued in June 1935. When this prototype flew for the first time in 1937 it was found to be underpowered and the project shelved.

We have seen how the Air Corps was prevented from pursuing the development of long-range bombers, but The Boeing Company, builders of the XB-15 (Boeing Model 294), continued studies and by 1939 had evolved the Model 341, designed to carry a 2,200-lb bomb-load over a maximum range of 7,000 miles at more than 400 mph.

Then, in 1940, the air force advised manufacturers of their requirement for a "Hemisphere Defense Weapon" (even with Europe at war it was still long-range bombers for defence!) to have heavy defensive armament, armour protection, self-sealing fuel tanks and a maximum bomb-load of 16,000 lb. It was required to have a range in excess of 5,000 miles with a 2,000-lb bomb-load, which it was to carry at 400 mph.

Boeing lost no time in developing the design of their Model 341 to meet this specification. In competition with the product of three other companies, the Boeing aircraft (Model 345) was judged to be the best, and two prototypes were ordered, on August 24, 1940, under the designation XB-29. Following inspection of a mock-up in April 1941, construction of the XB-29s commenced, and on September 21, 1942, the first of these flew.

Thus, the aircraft which in its developed state was to dominate the latter stages of war in the Pacific, and to carry destruction to the Japanese homeland, took the air slightly less than three years before final victory.

The final link in our chain of events had originated even before war had been declared in Europe, for during the period 1934–1939, scientific researchers had discovered that when certain atoms—and in particular those of uranium—were bombarded by neutrons, a new type of atomic disintegration occurred. It seemed possible that, under certain circumstances, a chain reaction could be initiated which would release an enormous quantity of energy in a very short time, thus creating an immensely powerful explosion.

Italian physicist Enrico Fermi, awarded a Nobel Prize in 1938 for experiments on artificial radioactivity by neutron bombardment, became a Professor at Columbia University in 1939. Continuing his research, he was soon able to demonstrate that fission of uranium could produce a chain reaction.

Aware that physicists in Germany were pursuing similar research, he tried to make the US Navy Department aware of the potential dangers. Unsuccessful, he turned to an associate—Leo Szilard—who was in a position to approach Albert Einstein. On August 2, 1939, Einstein wrote to advise President Roosevelt that: "In the course of the last four months, it has been made probable—through the work of Joliot in France as well as Fermi and Szilard in America—that it may become possible to set up nuclear chain reactions in a large mass of uranium, by which vast amounts of power and large quantities of new radium-like elements would be generated. Now it appears almost certain that this could be achieved in the immediate future.

"This new phenomenon would also lead to the construction of bombs, and it is conceivable—though much less certain—that extremely powerful bombs of a new type may thus be constructed."

So began investigation into the possible use of atomic energy to create an all-powerful bomb. Similar work was being conducted in the United Kingdom and, after America's entry into the war, scientists in both countries collaborated closely on the project.

Almost a year later, the certainty of success became apparent when the atomic pile, built in Chicago under the scientific direction of Enrico Fermi, went critical for the first time on December 2, 1942.

On that day, by means of what is now a historic telephone call, programme co-ordinator Arthur H. Compton advised Fermi's success to controller of the project, James B. Conant:

"The Italian navigator has landed in the New World," he said.

"How were the natives?" came Conant's reply.

"Very friendly."

Thus, by December 2, 1942, a little less than twelve months from America's participation in World War II, the die had been cast so far as ultimate victory over Japan was concerned.

But before victory could be assured, there was almost three years of bitter fighting to come. Fighting in which the 5th, 7th, 13th and 20th Air Forces had a vital rôle to play. It was, primarily, as the 7th Air Force put it somewhat succinctly: "Just one damned island after another". But fanatical Japanese resistance meant there was no short route to victory: each island became the scene of a major battle; each island lost to Japan brought the Americans a little nearer to the homeland. The perimeter of defence was shrinking slowly in a war of attrition that, by virtue of America's vast productive resources, slowly but inevitably favoured the West.

The one weapon which offered a shortcut was the Boeing B-29 Super-fortress, which began to enter service in mid-1943. But, at that time, it had a combat radius of only 1,600 miles, and the US held no bases near enough to Japan for its deployment.

There were two alternatives. First, to base the B-29s in India, where they could be staged through China: this implied attack capability in early 1944, but with the disadvantage of immense logistic problems. Second, to operate from bases in the Mariana Islands, some 1,500 miles south-east of the main Japanese island of Honshu. These islands were, however, occupied by the enemy and the date of their availability a matter of conjecture.

The former alternative was chosen, pending occupation of the Marianas, but it soon became apparent that the difficulties were far greater than had been estimated, involving the construction of huge air bases both in India and China. When the first B-29s began to arrive in India, early in April 1944, to form 20th Bomber Command, they discovered that activity against the enemy was the least of their worries.

Happily, the 20th was commanded by a logistics expert, Maj. Gen. Kenneth B. Wolfe, and this officer soon found full employment for his talents. It involved the carriage by air of the enormous quantities of materials, equipment and supplies to complete the bases in China and make them fit for their task: *en route* lay the Himalayas, the highest mountain range in the world. By the time that the B-29s could begin operation from the Marianas, they had completed considerably more transport than bombing sorties, for statistics show that for the eleven months that 20th Bomber Command had been based in India, only two operational sorties per aircraft were flown each month.

At last, in July 1944, after the 7th and 13th Air Forces had neutralised the Japanese-held island of Truk, in the Carolines, Army, Navy and Marines joined forces to capture Saipan, and in August Guam and Trinian fell to the Americans.

There followed a period of intense frustration for "Hap" Arnold, by then in command of the 20th Air Force, which had control of all B-29s. Until suitable bases had been built on the Marianas, his growing force of Superfortresses was impotent.

Eventually, on October 12, 1944, the first B-29 arrived at Saipan, piloted by Brig. Gen. Haywood S. Hansell, Jr. Sixteen days later an initial training operation, comprising 18 aircraft, was mounted against Truk, but met with little success. Training missions continued until November 24, when 111 B-29s began the campaign against the Japanese homeland.

This, the first bombing attack on Tokyo since the "Doolittle Raid", produced indifferent results, as did Hansell's daylight precision attacks on industrial targets which followed. One of the main factors which contributed to the disappointing results was the unusual and unpredictable weather conditions; turbulent high altitude winds made accurate bombing virtually impossible.

There was, too, an important psychological factor, provided by lack of an intermediate base where damaged aircraft could put down. It was not until B-24 Liberators of the 7th Air Force had pounded Iwo Jima for almost three weeks that the Marine Corps could land there, on February 19, 1945, fighting a desperate four-week battle to rid the island of enemy troops. Only then could engineers start construction of the emergency landing strips that, by the end of the war, had given sanctuary to nearly 2,400 Superfortresses and their crews.

Meanwhile, Arnold, impatient for success, replaced Hansell by Maj. Gen. Curtis E. LeMay. This officer, an experimenter by nature, mounted a few exploratory attacks against Japan in February 1945, using the incendiary bomb as prime weapon. In the following weeks, after careful evaluation of the pros and cons, he decided to utilise the Superfortresses in an entirely different way—in low-level night operations. He argued that this would not only permit carriage of a heavier bomb-load, primarily incendiaries, but since Japanese defence against night attack was poor, it was reasonable to assume a reduction in casualties.

The first of these attacks, carried out by 334 B-29s on the night of March 9, proved his strategy to be correct. More than 80,000 Japanese were killed, about a quarter of all the buildings in Tokyo destroyed, and no less than 15·8 square miles of the heart of the city was consumed by fire.

There was no looking back. The success of this operation blue-printed the fire-bomb campaign which, within only eleven days, eliminated 32 square miles of buildings in the industrial areas of Tokyo, Nagoya, Osaka and Kobe. By the end of the war Superforts had dropped 145,000 tons of bombs on Japan and destroyed 105 square miles in the centre of the six most important industrial cities. But this is anticipating the finale.

The thunder of the B-29s, the unearthly scream of the canisters of incendiaries that came plummeting down, the roar of flames: these were but a Wagnerian overture to the final act.

On August 6, the B-29 *Enola Gay*, piloted by Col. Paul Tibbetts, Jr, flying over Hiroshima at about 30,000 feet, dropped the world's first operational atomic bomb on the teeming city below. Over 4 square miles of buildings were destroyed by blast and fire and some 80,000 people killed—a total which rose ultimately to reach nearly 140,000 as others succumbed to their injuries or the effects of radiation.

Three days later, the important shipbuilding city of Nagasaki received similar treatment when the B-29 *Bock's Car*, piloted by Maj. Charles W. Sweeney, dropped a second plutonium bomb. Damage and casualties were less here than at Hiroshima, largely due to the fact that the city was spread over a series of hills and valleys, thus affording a measure of protection.

The following day, Japanese leaders realised that further resistance was futile and decided on immediate surrender. On September 2, 1945, aboard the battleship USS *Missouri*, General MacArthur received the Japanese envoys for the formal ceremony of surrender.

Air power had won a mighty victory: for the first time in military history an enemy had surrendered without invasion of its territory by land!

Lasting Peace

. . . With malice towards none; with charity for all; with firmness in the right, let us strive on to finish the work we are in; . . . to do all which may achieve and cherish a just and lasting peace, among ourselves and with all nations.

Abraham Lincoln. 2nd Inaugural Address, March 4, 1865

THE CROWDS that had thronged Times Square on V-J Day must have represented a fair cross-section of the American peoples. And, like a cross-section of humanity from any country in the world, they reacted in their many different ways to the realisation of victory.

Colour came from banners, streamers, best dresses, waving flags. Movement, too, as dancers jostled with the swaying crowds and younger citizens indulged in good-natured horse-play. Noise, inevitably: compounded of music, voices in song, laughter and cheers.

And there were those whose eyes glistened with the tears of pride: and those whose tears betokened different, deeper and more personal feelings.

Their many reactions, their dissimilarity in background, breeding, wealth—even colour—were inconsequential. They had, as a united nation, just won a great victory: so resounding a victory that they could, as a united nation, sit back and enjoy a lasting peace. For who dare raise a hand against the terrible deterrent of the atomic bomb that was theirs to wield.

Above all, they were united in a common thought, that within a short moment of time their husbands, sons and lovers would be hurrying back from the far corners of the earth: and if not, they wanted to know why.

It was an all-talking, singing and dancing version of 1919 all over again, and experience—dusty and neglected on the shelf of time—had taught neither government nor people a single useful lesson.

As in 1919, military authorities were unable to resist the dual pressures of public and treasury for rapid demobilisation. On V-J Day the USAAF had numbered about 2,253,000 personnel. Within little more than four months only 888,769 remained: by the end of May 1947 the mighty Army Air Force had shrunk to a mere 303,000 men. Effective combat units, totalling 218 at V-J Day, were reduced to but two in December

1946. True, at that time, the Air Force had 52 combat groups on paper: but of these, only two were effective.

Between September 1945 and March 1947, as the United States withdrew from military responsibility throughout the world, they left troops only in Germany, Japan and at a few strategic outposts. Their hasty exodus left undefended large areas of immediate importance to the Eastern bloc: ripe for occupation and development, they were quickly but roughly cultivated and sown with the seeds of Communism.

Great Britain, which had given its all to the restoration of peace, was no longer able, either militarily or economically, to play its traditional rôle of maintaining the balance of power in Europe and Asia.

Thus, by 1947, both military and political leaders in the West were aware of a developing impasse, to which the name of "Cold War" was applied. America responded to the situation by initiating help for countries threatened by aggression and, through the Marshal Plan, brought economic aid to war-ravaged Europe. Such action did much to stem the rate of Communist expansion, backed as it was by the implied threat of American military power, in particular the deterrent effect of the atomic bomb. Since, at that time, this weapon could be deployed only by the USAAF, this force was, in effect, the very cornerstone of American military power.

In considering the ability of the USAAF to fulfil such a rôle, leaders like Arnold and Spaatz were aware that the wheel had turned full circle and that, however bitter the truth, the Air Force was once again completely unfitted to accept the responsibility thrust upon it.

When Spaatz had become commanding general of the Air Force in 1946, he had been fortified only by the knowledge of the Air Staff's intention to rebuild, as quickly as possible, the combat strength of his force. He was sufficiently farsighted to realise that, in view of the fundamental importance of the air arm, it was but a matter of time before this became independent.

He began, therefore, to make preparation for that event, which three generations of Air Force leaders had fought to make fact, beginning with the creation of Strategic Air, Tactical Air and Air Defense Commands.

There had been others with foresight too, for even while the nations had been locked in combat, isolated members of Congress had introduced bills calling for an independent air force. Then, in 1944, the Joint Chief of Staff had appointed a committee to examine three basic defence organisations: (i) two departments: War and Navy; (ii) three departments: War, Navy and Air; or (iii) a single department: Defence.

Their recommendation, after ten months of intensive study and examination, was for a single department of armed forces, with three co-ordinate branches.

A further committee, sponsored by the Department of the Navy, while approving reorganisation of the nation's defence into three forces, did not agree with a single defence department.

Outwardly there appeared to be unity of purpose, but within was a bitter Navy versus Air Force controversy similar to that which Trenchard, in Britain, had fought against so valiantly in the years that followed World War I.

Thrust and counter-thrust continued until Presidential pressure to resolve the arguments resulted in Army and Navy leaders proposing a unification scheme to Congress in January 1947. It offered concessions to the Navy, by allowing for inclusion of aviation units and the Marine Corps into that service. Finally, the National Security Act of 1947 became law on July 26, creating the civilian position of Secretary of the Air Force—to be filled by Presidential appointment—and establishment of the United States Air Force. Executive Order 9877, signed by President Truman immediately after approval of the National Security Act, detailed the specific functions of the USAF.

Ceremony only was required to bring fulfilment of the hopes of autonomy that had been born almost forty years earlier.

On September 18, 1947, W. Stuart Symington was sworn in as the first Secretary of the Air Force: eight days later its first Chief of Staff took the oath, General Carl Spaatz. A proud moment, indeed, for the man who 18 years earlier had etched his name in Air Corps history with the endurance flight of the *Question Mark*.

If Spaatz had any moment free to indulge in nostalgia, *Question Mark* was an appropriate theme. At that moment, how best to reorganise the USAF to meet its worldwide commitments was one big question mark.

Great advantage lay in the fact that there was no break in the administrative chain. Headquarters USAF was new in name only. And Spaatz soon found that in Symington he had acquired the right man at the right time. Between them they began to fashion a sound and enduring organisational structure for the Air Force, drawing upon the experience and close co-operation of Gen. Hoyt S. Vandenburg, Lt. Gen. Lauris Norstad and Brig. Gen. William F. McKee, to achieve positive and rapid results.

Then, in mid-1948, just as they were getting into their stride, came indications of an even deeper freeze in the Cold War: so rapid, in fact, there seemed immediate danger of a new shooting war. On June 25 a teleprinter message from the Russian Zone of Berlin advised that: "The Transport Division of the Soviet Military Administration is compelled to halt all passenger and freight traffic to and from Berlin tomorrow at 0600 hours because of technical difficulties. . . ."

To understand the situation one must remember that, at the end of World War II, Berlin had become virtually an island within Germany, surrounded by the Russian Zone. Britain, France and the United States occupied West Berlin, the Russians East Berlin. Fortunately, although the Russians could close all surface routes to West Berlin, the Western Powers had been guaranteed free access to the city via three air corridors. Thus, when earlier in 1948 the Russians had temporarily closed the land routes, a limited airlift of passengers and freight had been carried out by US aircraft over a period of eleven days.

There was little doubt that by these new tactics the Soviet Union hoped to force the Western Powers to withdraw from Berlin. They did not reckon with the resolution of Gen. Lucius D. Clay, the US military governor and his British and French counterparts, who decided immediately to sustain the city by air.

Lt. Gen. Curtis E. LeMay, then commander of the United States Air Forces in Europe (USAFE) was asked to initiate an airlift into Berlin, responding with such speed that by the following day Douglas C-47 Skytrain cargo aircraft, better known as "Gooney Birds", had delivered 80 tons of urgently needed flour, milk and medical supplies. Satisfactory as this was, at such short notice, it was a mere drop in the ocean.

The two million civilian inhabitants of West Berlin, together with the occupying military forces, were estimated to require no less than 13,500 tons of supplies daily to meet normal consumption. At the very least, to provide an absolute minimum of subsistence, 1,500 tons would need to be flown in every twenty-four hours.

Even while his small force of C-47s was making its first delivery, LeMay hastily summoned assistance from Headquarters USAF. Within four weeks, Brig. Gen. Joseph Smith, initially in command of the operation, could deploy a total of 105 C-47s and 54 C-54 Skymasters, able to carry a maximum of 1,500 tons daily: British Yorks and Dakotas provided an additional 750 tons per day, but it was clear that much greater efforts would be required as winter approached and the demand for solid fuel became more urgent.

Anticipating this, on July 23 Gen. Vandenburg ordered the Military Air Transport Service (MATS) to send eight additional squadrons of C-54s to Germany, and these began to arrive at a rate of two squadrons a week. The first eighteen to join the Berlin shuttle helped boost the US airlift to 2,000 tons on July 31.

Airlift Task Force (Provisional), formed on July 29, had Maj. Gen. William H. Tunner in command, and by September his C-47s were replaced by almost 300 C-54s, together with some Douglas C-74 Globemasters and a small number of Fairchild C-82 Flying Boxcars. Reinforced by an average 140 British military and civil aircraft, as well as others operated by the French, it became possible to maintain a daily airlift of around 5,000 tons.

The organisation of such a mass of aircraft within the confines of the narrow air corridors was a tremendous task, imposing great responsibility upon air traffic control which derived much of its efficiency from the expert staff supplied by MATS technical service and the Civil Aeronautics Administration.

As tonnage increased, congestion at Tempelhof and Gatow airports became so acute that a new airfield at Tegel, in the French sector, was built by German men and women who laboured day and night levelling rubble gathered from the bomb-shattered buildings of Berlin. On December 7, 1948, their efforts were rewarded when the first aircraft came in to land there.

Winter weather, some of the worst experienced in Europe for many years, brought a serious drop in cargoes delivered and at one period it was estimated that only a single week's supply of coal remained in the city.

But as soon as the weather began to show some improvement tonnage soared to new levels: 171,000 tons in January 1949; 152,000 tons in February; 196,000 tons in March; and a superb 234,500 tons in April. The record for a single day was established on Easter Sunday, April 16, when no less than 12,940 tons were off-loaded in Berlin.

In the face of such determination it is hardly surprising that the Russians found a solution to their "technical difficulties" and, on May 12, reopened the surface routes to Berlin. Just to "make sure", the airlift continued until reserve stocks in the city had reached an adequate level and then, gradually, the winged fleet of cargo ships was withdrawn.

The Berlin Airlift had been conducted with a loss of 51 lives, 17 aircraft and had cost the USAF and US Navy between them a total estimated at $181·3 million; but in many respects this was lives and money devoted to a worthwhile purpose. It had demonstrated quite clearly to the Communist bloc that the Western Powers were determined to preserve peace at any cost; it had provided a first class exercise in team work for air forces of the West; and it had been a unique proving ground for the utilisation of massed air transport for civil, rather than military, needs.

During the period of the Berlin Airlift it had been appreciated that a Russian threat to Western Europe might not always be contained so easily. This realisation hastened formation of the North Atlantic Treaty Organisation (NATO), in April 1949. As a leading member of NATO the United States had to provide a large share towards the defence of Western Europe, and this resulted in strong USAF tactical air units being based in several NATO countries, principally Britain, France and Germany.

Such action brought some restoration of the balance of power in

Europe and the Communists were not long in seeking a new area of challenge. This time their choice fell upon Korea which, since 1919, had been regarded as an integral part of the Japanese Empire. At Potsdam, in 1945, it had been agreed that when Japan was defeated the Soviet Union would accept the surrender of Japanese troops north of the 38th parallel, American forces those south of this line of demarcation.

The West had never intended that the 38th parallel should become, in effect, an "iron curtain" separating the country into Communist and anti-communist states and so, while American forces in the south had assisted in peaceful reconstruction schemes, the Russians busied themselves by imposing Communism in the north, and helped to train a North Korean Army.

A general election in South Korea in 1948 resulted in the foundation of the Republic of Korea, recognised by all but the Soviet bloc as the lawful government of the country as a whole. "Elections" in the North produced the Korean People's Republic, blessed by the Communists, and following establishment of which Soviet forces were withdrawn, leaving only a limited number of technicians. In the South, American forces also left the country, leaving behind a small advisory group.

The scene was set and here, in the early hours of June 25, 1950, North Korean infantry spearheaded by Soviet-built tanks streamed over the border to attack the Republic of Korea. The Western Powers, both shocked and unprepared, realised at once that the fuse of a potential third world war had been lit. Throughout the world ordinary men and women held their breath in fear as they wondered whether the somewhat shaky United Nations held the necessary power to stamp out this fuse before the resulting explosion embroiled them all in a new and far more norrifying war.

President Truman, at any rate, did not hesitate to take immediate and positive action, ordering the USAF to support the Republic until such time as the United Nations could or would act. Response from the Air Force was equally quick and on the following day they were able to provide air cover for the Port of Inchon where Americans still in Korea were being evacuated by sea.

On June 27 transport aircraft of the 5th Air Force's 374th Troop Carrier Wing began air evacuation of the remaining Americans from Kimpo Airfield, while North American F-82 Twin Mustang fighters of the 5th Air Force, operating from Itazuke, Japan, provided air cover and, in the process, shot down three Yak fighters to produce the USAF's first victories of the Korean War.

Prime task was to establish a base in an area unlikely to be overrun by the Communists, and Pusan was chosen at Korea's southernmost tip. Here were based the North American P-51 Mustangs and Lockheed

F-80C Shooting Star jet fighters which, together, took the brunt of the early combat sorties. They were joined there by two of Strategic Air Command's B-29 bomber groups, and in the two months following their arrival they succeeded in destroying practically all of the worthwhile military targets then available to them in North Korea.

These early successes began to give the impression that victory was at hand and then, on November 26, 1950, events suddenly took a new and far more serious turn for the worse as Red Chinese forces poured across the Manchurian border to join the conflict.

The demands upon the USAF multiplied at once, but it was no easy task to conjure a robust rabbit from a hat that had shrunk to almost nothing. To meet the situation air units were reshuffled all around the world, reserves recalled and tactical aircraft of an earlier generation freed from their mothballs and put back into service.

The immediate problem to be resolved was the provision of adequate air cover for the United Nations' forces, outnumbered and hard-pressed as they made a fighting withdrawal to the south. In this the Air Force was successful, aided by some units of the US Navy and as the Chinese advanced further south their lines of communication became so attenuated that it was possible for the B-26 and B-29 bombers to cause such serious disruption to the enemy's supplies that, once again, the pendulum seemed to swing in favour of the United Nations.

It was but a temporary respite, for as 1950 drew to a close increasing numbers of Russian-built MiG-15 jet fighters began to appear on the scene and these proved more than a match for the combat aircraft that the USAF could put into the air to oppose them. With Communist domination of the daylight skies over Korea, the daylight bombing sorties which had been paying such rich dividends proved far too costly to continue and made it necessary for the B-29s to be deployed by night, operating from bases as far away as Guam, Japan and Okinawa.

Then, at this critical period, the 4th Fighter Interceptor Wing which was equipped with the North American F-86 Sabre jet fighter became operational and their arrival in Korea was providential for, though slightly inferior to the MiG-15 in performance, particularly at altitude, the skill of the USAF pilots was such that they were able quickly to record initial victories when they destroyed four MiGs on December 17. Almost simultaneously, the third USAF jet fighter to serve in Korea became operational with the 27th Fighter Escort Wing. This was the Republic F-84D Thunderjet, prime duty of which was to protect the B-29s as they penetrated enemy air space.

Faced with growing opposition from the USAF, the Communists soon realised their own air support to be inadequate. To make it more potent they needed advanced airfields from which their MiG fighters could operate and, without delay, embarked upon a big programme of airfield construction, beginning with four bases for the jet fighters some 70 miles south of the Yalu. USAF aircraft kept these activities under careful surveillance and, when they were nearing completion, Superfortresses cratered the runways and destroyed buildings and other installations. The Chinese redoubled their efforts to rebuild the bases: again USAF reconnaissance aircraft kept a close eye on the situation and, at the appropriate moment, destroyed them—a cat and mouse affair that continued until finally the enemy gave up in despair.

By the spring of 1951 the production lines of the American aircraft industry had gathered momentum, once again starting to provide immense quantities of aircraft so that the USAF were able to dominate the skies of Korea. As this armada ruthlessly pounded enemy troop concentrations, it soon became clear to the Communists that despite the immense manpower reserves of Red China, there was a limit to the losses that could be tolerated without the risk of political strife between the Soviet Union and China. Accordingly, on June 23, 1951, the Soviet delegate to the United Nations made a proposal for cease-fire discussions to be initiated.

Unfortunately, this did not end the war, which dragged on for rather more than two years, a period in which the USAF were far from inactive. On the contrary, they began an intensive programme of interdiction, blasting railways, bridges, roads, war industries and storage centres. Targets which, for political reasons, had escaped the attention of the USAF earlier in the conflict now became subject matter for their briefing rooms. For example, the complex of hydro-electric power plants in North Korea which together supplied practically all of the country's electric power, were virtually eliminated in three days of bombing.

The F-84 Thunderjets proved themselves to be ideal for this type of attack, and when it was decided to hit at the irrigation system of the paddy fields, from which came the staple diet of the Koreans and, incidentally, fed also the Red Army, these aircraft were chosen for the task. On May 13, 1953, 59 F-84s attacked the Toksan dam: when it collapsed, the resulting flood destroyed bridges, railway tracks and roads for almost 100 miles north of Pyongyang. This success led to a series of similar raids, and it seems highly possible that wholesale destruction of the basic agricultural system of the North Koreans hurried their decision to sign the cease-fire agreement on July 27, 1953.

Once again air power had won peace: the forces of the United Nations, and in the main the air forces of the United States, had completed a successful fire-brigade action, confining the flames of battle to a relatively small area and, by gradually cooling them down, had prevented escalation of the conflict into another world war. Even the enemy, in the shape of the chief North Korean delegate to the truce talks had to admit, however reluctantly, that the USAF had played a major part in the defeat of his forces.

Post-mortems are valuable in many fields: that held on the cause of war in Korea left little doubt that, encouraged by the run-down of America's military strength—particularly her air force—the Communist bloc had considered there was little real danger in resorting to open warfare in Korea.

Awareness of this fact triggered off a new growth of military might in the United States. The USAF was authorised to expand to 143 combat wings by 1954 and this, in turn, initiated a drive for new and better combat aircraft, and the "century series" of jet fighters, beginning with the F-100 Super Sabre, F-101 Voodo and the F-102 Delta Dart, emanate from this period. The prototype of the B-58 Hustler, first of the supersonic jet bombers, was ordered at this time, and the British-designed Martin B-57 (Canberra) jet bomber began to enter service in quantity.

There was the beginning, too, of reinforcement from an entirely different source. The closing stages of World War II had witnessed deployment of the world's first strategic ballistic missile—the German V-2 rocket. The USAAF had been quick to react to the potential of such weapons and, before the war's end, had started missile research and development. This continued during the early post-war years and throughout the 1950s, and initial studies were directed towards the design and development of four main classes of this weapon:

(i) An air-to-air weapon, later known as the guided aircraft rocket (GAR).

(ii) Surface-to-air weapons, or long-range interceptor missiles (IM).

(iii) Air-to-surface, or stand-off weapons, called a guided aircraft missile (GAM).

(iv) Surface-to-surface weapons which were classed as tactical missiles (TM), for the support of ground forces, or strategic missiles (SM) for long-range deployment.

The USAAF began development of two long-range strategic missiles soon after World War II had ended: the SM-62 Snark and the SM-64 Navaho, known then as pilotless bombers. Of these, only the first—a subsonic intercontinental weapon—became operational hardware and served as an interim weapon during the period in which the whole concept of missile attack and defence was being argued and developed.

Initially the Air Force did not possess a warhead small enough or powerful enough to make the deployment of these weapons a worthwhile proposition. The breakthrough came early in 1954 when advances in thermonuclear physics made the construction of such a weapon a practical proposition. This followed closely upon a report by the Strategic Missiles Committee, headed by Dr John von Neumann, which having investigated thoroughly intelligence information and other factors, were able to forecast that within five years America's ranking in the missile league would be such that, without intense national effort, the country would be in mortal danger.

Air Force response to this warning was immediate, and weight and urgency were added in September 1955 when President Eisenhower gave top priority to the development of an intercontinental ballistic missile (ICBM).

In order to carry out the necessary programme, the USAF created the Western Development Division of Air Research and Development Command (ARDC), headed by Brig. Gen. B. A. Schriever, while the Ballistic Missile Center of Air Material Command was set up for procurement, production and logistical support. The initial projects of this unique service organisation were the SM-65 Atlas ICBM and an intermediate-range ballistic missile (IRBM), the SM-75 Thor.

Meanwhile, the Air Force proper had been going about the task of creating and equipping its 143 combat wings. In fact, this had resolved into a total of 137, comprising 54 planned for Strategic Air Command, 34 for Air Defense Command, 38 for Tactical Air Command and 11 Troop Carrier Wings, all of which were due to be operational by the summer of 1957. If the Communist fraternity had hoped that termination of the Korean War would bring about a 1918- or 1945-type cut-back in air power, they were doomed to disappointment.

The cost, of course, was immense; but there was no obvious alternative. Peace hinged upon deterrence, and deterrence implied a need to maintain the capability of immediate and massive retaliation. This was the task of Strategic Air Command which, in 1955, began to arm with the B-52 Stratofortress jet bomber, an aircraft that had been developed following the success of the B-47 Stratojet, which was the first swept-wing jet bomber built in quantity for any air force. When the B-52 became available in quantity, it represented the most vital weapon in the USAF's armoury. The importance lay in its potential ability to deliver a nuclear weapon to any target in the world.

Air Defense Command became integrated into the Continental Air Defense Command, comprising Army, Navy and Air Force units under the operational control of an Air Force officer, and responsible for the defence of the North American continent. Thus, for the first time in its history, America gained a nationwide air defence system which consisted of a co-ordinated blend of early-warning ground radar, airborne early-warning aircraft, airborne interceptor patrols, as well as more conventional anti-aircraft units which, as the missile programme developed, became unconventional as they were reinforced by USAF ground-to-air interceptor missiles.

Tactical Air Command, created as a mobile strike force, was equipped to deal with "brush fire" wars, and soon became operationally capable of deploying immense strength at any global point where a spark of aggression might burst into active flame. It had also gained the capability of deploying a tactical missile, the TM-61 Martin Matador, which could carry either a conventional or nuclear warhead.

And so, as 1956 drew to a close, there was little doubt that the United States Air Force was stronger than its descendants had ever been. It was true also that its deterrent effect was a prime factor in the maintenance of a costly if uneasy peace: but there were few in the West who could argue that it was not worth while; or could offer a better or cheaper solution. Only time would prove whether the concept of deterrence would be adequate to ensure the desire of all the American peoples— indeed, of ordinary people throughout the length and breadth of our teeming world—a heartfelt desire for the maintenance of a lasting peace.

Any Price

. . . Let every nation know, whether it wishes us well or ill, that we shall pay any price, bear any burden, meet any hardship, support any friend, oppose any foe to ensure the survival and success of liberty. . . .

John F. Kennedy. Inaugural Address

NEW YEAR'S DAY, 1957, must have seemed a pretty fair day to any average citizen of the United States with time to pause and consider national affairs. On the credit side of the ledger trade was buoyant generally; the much-respected "Ike" had been re-elected for a new term; the ugliness and unpleasantries of the anti-Communist risings in Hungary and Anglo-French participation in the Suez crisis were behind them; and with the security offered by a Navy, Army and Air Force that had never been stronger in times of "peace" there appeared to be few serious worries.

More significantly, however, a deeper-thinking citizen could be excused for considering that the debit side of the ledger was rather frightening. A picture of flourishing economy was overshadowed by the weak position of the farming community; Eisenhower's re-election was principally a personal triumph—there was little enthusiasm for the policies of the party he represented; and disquieting pointers of unrest throughout the world voiced the question of whether the armed forces were equipped adequately to enforce the maintenance of peace.

A clairvoyant of unprecedented ability might well have doubted the truth of his own prognostications if, at the beginning of 1957, he could have foretold accurately the cost of attempting to keep up with—or a little ahead of—the Joneskis in the decade ahead.

President Kennedy's "any price" of 1961 was really nothing new: his statement was fundamentally a reiteration of American policy that had been born twenty years earlier, at Pearl Harbor.

What then, for the Air Force, was "any price"?

In terms of speed it involved the series of "X" aircraft which added immeasurably to the nation's storehouse of aerodynamic knowledge. Way back in 1947 Capt. Charles ("Chuck") Yeager had been first man to exceed the speed of sound (Mach 1·0) in the Bell X-1; in 1954 Major Arthur Murray had taken the X-1A to an altitude of 94,000 feet; and before Capt. Milburn G. Apt crashed to his death in the X-2 in September 1956 he had flown at a reported 2,178 mph.

The North American X-15 programme took over in 1955, and by July 1962 Major Robert White had taken the X-15A to a height of 59·6 miles, thus qualifying for US Astronaut's "wings" by travelling more than 50 miles above the Earth's surface. Near the end of this decade, on November 18, 1966, Major Pete Knight flew the X-15A-2 at a speed equivalent to 4,250 mph.

The world speed record over a 15/25-km course at unlimited altitude was captured by Col. Robert L. Stephens and Lt. Col. Daniel Andre flying the unique YF-12A experimental interceptor. First-ever over 2,000 mph speed record, these Air Force pilots still held the record at 2,070·102 mph at the time these words were being written.

This decade recorded also the introduction into service of the Convair B-58 Hustler, the Air Force's first supersonic bomber, capable of a speed of nearly 1,400 mph. Another costly high-speed item was the construction of two North American XB-70 Valkyries, prototypes of a unique tail-first delta-wing aircraft designed to meet a USAF requirement for a strategic bomber, able to carry a nuclear weapon over a target-and-back distance of about 7,500 miles at a speed of Mach 3·0. Intended originally to replace the B-52s in service in the mid-1960s, it became the victim of policy changes and only the two XB-70A prototypes were built.

In terms of fire-power, the missile programmes initiated during the early post-war years began to pay off during this decade, providing completely new and lethal weapons to arm the Air Force's aircraft. Amongst these was the McDonnell Douglas Genie, an unguided air-to-air rocket-powered missile with a nuclear warhead, which was used for the first-ever test firing of an air-to-air nuclear missile on July 19, 1957.

A more important missile was the Hughes Falcon, first air-to-air guided weapon adopted by the USAF and which, in its various forms, has become standard armament of the force's all-weather interceptors. In addition, a number of missiles developed for and in service with the US Navy, had also entered service with the USAF.

To increase the offensive capability of Strategic Air Command's B-52 fleet, the North American Hound Dog stand-off missile was developed and the Stratofortresses could also carry several decoy missiles known as Quail which, because of their speed and the electronic countermeasures equipment carried, were able to confuse an enemy's defence system by simulating a B-52 in flight.

On the ground the USAF was able to deploy the Boeing Bomarc, the world's first long-range surface-to-air interceptor missile, having a guidance system integrated with the Semi-Automatic Ground Environment (SAGE) network which was brought into operation in 1957. This system made it possible to control, to the best possible advantage, the men, machines and missiles concerned with the defence of America.

In terms of a missile-based deterrent, this decade saw introduction of Mace, a medium-range weapon carrying either conventional or nuclear warhead. This was, of course, secondary to the ICBMs of which Atlas was first into service, an initial successful test firing being accomplished on December 17, 1957. Little less than a year later a fully equipped Atlas made an accurate 6,325-mile flight to provide Strategic Air Command with a valuable interim weapon. It was followed by Titan which, like its predecessor, had a power plant composed of liquid-propellant rockets.

Most important of the deterrent missiles was the third to enter service, the solid-propellant powered Minuteman ICBM. This power plant gave the weapon significant advantages, for it was smaller, lighter, more easily dispersed and cheaper to construct. Far more important, it required less personnel for its operation and maintenance and could be launched by remote control within seconds of a commital decision. By mid-June 1965 a total of 800 of these missiles were deployed in underground silos, forming five SAC Missile Wings under the operational control of the 15th Air Force.

By 1959, cost of the USAF's ballistic missile programme was approaching an annual $2 billion, involved almost 1,500 Air Force administrative officers, some 14,000 scientists and the participation of nearly 76,000 workers in twenty-two industries. It was clear that the cost of "any price" was becoming astronomical—and what of the space programme in which the USAF had become involved deeply?

By the end of the 6th decade the Air Force had provided the major portion of the national space effort and some 67 per cent of all launch vehicles used from the beginning of the space programme were USAF systems launched by Air Force crews. Almost 95 per cent of post-launch tracking and control was provided by USAF bases around the world.

The development of ballistic missiles had forged the USAF's link with space activities, since it was Air Force missiles that had provided much of the initial launch capability. It was not until April 1, 1961, however, that the Ballistic Systems and Space Systems Divisions of the newly formed Air Force Systems Command was created, the formation of which may be regarded as the true start of a military space programme—a Command and a programme whose formation had been accelerated by events that had occurred almost four years earlier.

Not the American nation alone, but citizens of the Western world in general, had comforted themselves throughout the "cold war" years in the belief that the West held such an enormous lead over the Communists in the fields of atomic and missile research that there was virtually no danger of any major conflict developing.

This fragile bubble of comfort was shaken in August 1957 when the Soviet Union announced they had an ICBM in service: it was shattered rudely two months later when, on October 4, they successfully launched their *Sputnik 1* satellite into orbit around the Earth, thus revealing that Soviet scientists had gained a completely unexpected lead over the West. Confirmation of their technical lead came on the third day of the following month when *Sputnik 2* was placed in Earth orbit, carrying a payload of around half a ton, bringing realisation of the enormous power of the booster rockets that the Communists had available to them.

Four days later, President Eisenhower outlined—for anyone in the West still clinging to their rose-tinted spectacles—the theat to delicately-poised East-West relations imposed by the Sputnik launchings:

"... Their current military significance lies in the advanced techniques and the competence in military technology they imply ... the Soviets continue to concentrate on the development of war-making weapons and supporting industries. This, as well as their political attitude in all international affairs, seems to warn us that Soviet expansionist aims have not ended. I must say to you, in all gravity ... it is entirely possible that in the years ahead we could fall behind (in military capability) unless we now face up to certain pressing requirements and set out to meet them at once."

On the United States, most advanced of the Western nations in missile technology, fell the responsibility of maintaining superiority in space. This meant, inevitably, that the Air Force had a major part to play.

Well behind in the space race, it was not until a year later, on October 11, 1958, that the USAF was able to chalk up its first "first", when a Thor-Able launch vehicle boosted *Pioneer 1* 71,000 miles out towards the Moon, man's deepest penetration of space at that time. Two months later an Atlas B booster put the world's first communications satellite into orbit and this, through the medium of a taped message, broadcast Christmas and New Year greetings from President Eisenhower to the peoples of the world.

The next two years was a period of intense effort in which American scientists and engineers made every possible endeavour to reduce the Soviet lead in space technology. It was also a period during which the USAF recorded no fewer than 46 space launches. Theirs was a battle against disheartening failures; but the resolution of all personnel involved slowly but surely turned uncertainty into reliability, and in the process they scored some impressive "firsts". These include the first satellite placed into a polar orbit, first photographs of the earth taken from space, and the first mid-air and ocean capsule recoveries.

But on April 12, 1961, the Russians once again shook the world by achieving the greatest of all firsts to that time, when Major Yuri Gagarin became first man to orbit the Earth, carried in the space ship *Vostok 1*.

It seemed that the Soviets had gained an enormous and unassailable lead.

For the USAF there followed the painstaking and time-consuming task of man-rating the Atlas booster, in the process of which they cemented a very close relationship with NASA. This partnership recorded its first major success when, on February 20, 1962, an Air Force Atlas D placed the Mercury capsule *Friendship 7* safely into Earth orbit, carrying within its confines the United States' first true astronaut, Marine Lt. Col. John H. Glenn. When the Mercury programme concluded, with the Mercury-Atlas 9 flight of May 15 and 16, 1963, when USAF Major LeRoy Gordon Cooper was in command, America was beginning to whittle back the Soviet lead.

There followed a nail-biting period while Titan II was being man-rated to provide a booster for the Gemini two-man capsule. It was a worthwhile period of patience, for the success of the Gemini programme finally closed the space gap between West and East. It began with the flight of Gemini 3 *Molly Brown* on March 23, 1965, carrying Lt. Col. Virgil I. Grissom, USAF, and Commander John W. Young, USN, on a completely successful three-orbit mission.

By the time the programme concluded there had been ten successful manned launches during which astronauts had walked in space, rendez-voused with Agena D targets or other Gemini craft, docked with target vehicles and, using their propulsion systems, had taken up new and world record orbital altitudes.

The programme terminated almost at the end of the decade, on November 11, 1966, when Gemini 12 commenced a highly successful four-day flight during which astronaut Maj. Edwin E. Aldrin, Jr, set a world's record for extra-vehicular activity, spending a total of five and a half hours outside Gemini.

There were other aspects related to space activity too, for with a future prospect of placing manned space stations in permanent orbit, the USAF initiated research into the feasibility of a vehicle that could orbit in space and yet fly more or less conventionally within the Earth's atmosphere. This led to development of the Northrop/NASA M2-F2 and HL-10 and the Martin Marietta X-23A and X-24A lifting-body vehicles, and experience gained with these revolutionary aircraft may well lead to development of the true space shuttle of the future.

But above all, what was "any price" in terms of the USAF's worldwide commitments?

First involvement of the decade had come in 1957 when the Communists attempted a takeover in Jordan. The following year there was fear of major trouble in the Middle East following assassination of King Faisal II of Iraq. At the request of the Lebanon government elements of the USAF's Tactical Air Force were rushed in, while C-130

Hercules transports of Military Air Transport Service carried infantry and Marine reinforcements into Beirut. A month later the situation had stabilised sufficiently for US forces to be withdrawn.

Seeking to take advantage of the world's temporary preoccupation with Middle East affairs, Chinese Communists began heavy bombardment of the islands of Quemoy and Matsu. They did not succeed in catching the Air Force sleeping, for Tactical Air Command immediately deployed units to Taiwan to offset this new threat to peace.

In mid-1960 the Congo became a trouble spot during early months of independence, starting the longest airlift in history—so much so that each round trip from Europe to the Congo was equivalent to 44 flights made during the Berlin Airlift. In a period of 14 months, MATS aircraft carried into Leopold 26,000 UN troops and 20 million pounds of cargo.

While the Middle East airlift was in operation new and serious trouble erupted in Berlin when the East Germans closed the border between East and West Berlin. To prepare for any new Soviet move in Europe the NATO countries immediately began a build-up of military power. In the United States this involved a call to active service for the Air National Guard and Air Force Reserve units and within weeks four National Guard squadrons of tactical fighters and their supporting elements had been deployed to Europe. The speed with which this defensive manoeuvre was carried out proved adequate to prevent the Communists from making any further moves in Europe, but the tension which developed was in no way relieved when East and West Berlin became permanently divided by the construction of the Berlin Wall.

Testing time for the American deterrent came in the autumn of the following year when, on October 14, 1962, USAF reconnaissance aircraft confirmed that intermediate-range missile sites were being constructed in Cuba. Here, clearly, was a new Soviet threat virtually upon America's own doorstep. Two days later, after service chiefs had considered the photographic evidence and its implications, President Kennedy ordered immediate deployment of the Navy, Army and Air Force to certain strategic positions, and all were instructed to stand by at the alert.

The USAF had an enormous task to encompass within a matter of days. Strategic Air Command B-47s and B-52s on airborne alert training flights worked in co-operation with the Navy, recording the track and position of all shipping in the Atlantic Ocean; simultaneously MATS began the task of airlifting vast quantities of men with their equipment and weapons to predetermined points of contingency.

Air Defense Command and Tactical Air Command were like a hive of bees, with fighters, reconnaissance and transport aircraft—together with thousands of men and their equipment—making for the south-eastern states as quickly as wings could carry them.

Finally, on October 22, the day President Kennedy had chosen to broadcast to the world—and in particular to the leaders of the Soviet Union—a clear statement of the government's policy and attitude, Strategic Air Command initiated a massive airborne alert for its Strato-fortresses. Those not airborne were on instantaneous ground alert and, at the same time, all her ICBM crews were placed at a similar state of readiness.

Thus, when the moment came for the President's broadcast, he was able to speak from a position of strength: the entire forces of the nation were keyed for action and within less time than it takes to read this sentence the frightening deterrent power of SAC could be let loose.

Kennedy's words came to a waiting world calmly and firmly:

". . . a strict quarantine . . . is being initiated. All ships of any kind bound for Cuba from whatever nation or port will, if found to contain cargoes of offensive weapons, be turned back. . . . I have directed the Armed Forces to prepare for any eventualities; and I trust that, in the interest of both the Cuban people and the Soviet technicians at the sites, the hazards to all concerned of continuing this threat will be recognised.

". . . It shall be the policy of this nation to regard any nuclear missile launched from Cuba against any nation in the Western Hemisphere as an attack by the Soviet Union on the United States, requiring a full retaliatory response upon the Soviet Union. . . ."

These were not the honeyed words of diplomacy: it was a clear, unequivocal statement of intent. Throughout the world people awaited the outcome, many in fear that the President had stepped over the threshold of prudence, that a nervous or trigger-happy individual on either side could spark off a nuclear war that would end civilisation as we know it.

As days passed without any statement from the Soviet Union tension mounted and then, almost as an anti-climax, it was learned that the Communists had backed down. The military installations in Cuba were dismantled, their missiles shipped back to Russia and the world began to breathe again.

This was a historic purchase for "any price": it was also a special validation for the "king's ransom" spent on bringing the Air Force to such a potential that there is little doubt it was a major factor in Russia's decision to withdraw her support from the Cubans.

Once again there was "peace" of the kind that we have now come to regard as normal, and events which followed were to a pattern that was becoming hackneyed. Once again trouble was brewing in the Far East.

To understand the situation we must take a look at the French colonial possessions known pre-war as Indo-China and comprising Cambodia,

Laos and the three provinces of Annam, Cochin-China and Tonking. During the war, under Japanese occupation, a strong nationalist movement had developed there, the most powerful group being the Communist-led Viet Minh.

With the war over, France wanted her colonies restored, but soon found that it would be necessary to fight for their return. War weary and quite unfitted to face up to a protracted and remote campaign, especially as she was employing the strategies of three decades earlier, it did not take long to discover that the upsurge of Communism was completely beyond her ability to contain. The Viet Minh had been well trained in the guerilla tactics of Mao Tse-tung, and this led to a gradual erosion of the French forces until, by early 1954, their casualties numbered almost 90,000. The last straw, so far as the French were concerned, came on May 7, 1954, when they surrendered some 16,000 men and their equipment at Diên Biên Phu.

Two months later, at Geneva, a 14-nation conference reached agreement to end the fighting. The three French provinces were divided into two states, known as North and South Vietnam, the 17th parallel representing the border between them. The Viet Minh were to occupy the north, France the south, and it was hoped that subsequent general elections would unite the country.

By the end of 1955 France had withdrawn all her troops from Vietnam, but this did little to quiet a confused situation compounded of political, economic, social and religious problems. Add to this civil strife between bands of guerillas, innumerable private armies disputing matters at gunpoint, and thousands of homeless refugees seeking sanctuary from someone—anyone—it was clear to the Western powers that the Communists would not delay long in exploiting the situation. This would mean, inevitably, that control of Vietnam would fall into their hands.

Only the United States was willing and able to oppose such a move, and they began by supplying military advisers and equipment to the Republic of Vietnam which had the Nationalist Ngo Dinh Diem as its President. This brought some stability to the situation in South Vietnam, but it was not long before small pockets of Viet Minh began to step up the guerilla warfare. American counter to this was reorganisation of the South Vietnamese army, making them more flexible and mobile to deal with this kind of action.

But with formation of the National Liberation Front of South Vietnam (Viet Cong) in December 1960, events assumed a more serious character, for prime aim of this organisation was the elimination of foreign interference in domestic affairs; a pistol pointed directly at the Americans.

In the four years which followed there was a steady build-up of the Viet Cong forces, while guerilla tactics increased in much the same proportion. To meet this the United States increased the number of advisory units in the South and began to base a growing number of more advanced aircraft there. But so far as the US was concerned the writing was on the wall, for all to see, when on August 2, 1964, units of the 7th Fleet, cruising outside the Communist-imposed 12-mile limit in the Gulf of Tonkin, were attacked by three North Vietnamese torpedo boats.

It was not until early in 1965, however, that President Lyndon B. Johnson decided to increase military pressure on the Viet Cong, starting in February, when Navy and Air Force aircraft began to attack military targets in the north. In March large numbers of American combat troops arrived in the country and began immediately to assist the hard-pressed Army of Vietnam (Arvin troops). At the end of 1965 Navy, Army and Air Force personnel in Vietnam totalled some 184,000: a year later this figure had almost doubled.

Inevitably, the USAF had to shoulder an immense task, and the dearly bought lessons of Korea, and other military incidents prior to Vietnam, proved invaluable in preparing the Air Force to fight what they came to regard as three separate wars.

The first of these was confined mainly to the area of the Mekong Delta, where Arvin troops were responsible for the ground fighting. Here the war became a bitter struggle, for it was not always easy to determine between friend and foe—not until it was too late. And here the battle was dominated by the activities of Forward Air Controllers (FACs) in their little Cessna O-1 Bird Dogs. Each FAC pilot, rather like a policeman on his beat, had an area of responsibility in which he was expected to know every detail of the landscape. As the FACs flew around looking for signs of the Viet Cong, they soon became expert at spotting above-average concentrations of men and sampans, or signs of new construction, and could call in an air or artillery strike within minutes.

Able to call upon a wide variety of aircraft and weapons, according to the target in prospect, FACs had control of fast, hard-hitting F-100s carrying napalm, phosphorus bombs, cluster bomb units, high-explosive bombs, rockets and Sidewinder, Sparrow or Bullpup missiles. They could also call in the armed helicopters, aircraft that came-of-age in Korea, and could now throw a deadly hail of fire. The Bird Dogs carried smoke rockets beneath their wings, and the FACs used these to indicate to USN or USAF aircraft just where they wanted a strike made, calling out corrections if their indicator was off target.

Another of the new tricks developed for a new kind of warfare involved the deployment of twin-engined Fairchild-Hiller C-123 transports in the rôle of chemical-spraying agricultural aircraft. In this case their hoppers were not charged with growth-promoting fertilisers; instead they carried chemicals to defoliate the living vegetation which provided cover for the guerillas. In the Delta area this was a particularly hazardous task, for the enemy could follow the approach of the C-123s for miles over the low coastal plain, giving them ample opportunity to prepare a warm welcome. Such was this greeting, in fact, that before the end of 1966 the crews of this squadron had earned no fewer than 27 Purple Hearts, a true indication of the hazards of low, vulnerable flight in the C-123s.

Astonishing as it may seem, the ageless and apparently indestructible DC-3 (C-47) had an important part to play in this area too. Armed with three mini-guns that were able to erupt with a combined 18,000 rounds per minute (300 rounds per second!) burst of fire, they were chosen because they were big enough to carry plenty of ammunition for the greedy guns, tough enough to take a lot of punishment, tall enough to give the gunners headroom in the fuselage, and slow enough to provide a stable platform for the guns. As they orbited the target in a lazy port bank they proved invaluable in pinning down the Viet Cong.

In this area, as in all others, helicopters proved invaluable for a host of tasks, including the carriage of troops, together with their equipment and supplies, evacuation of the wounded, the rescue of downed aircrew —and in many cases their aircraft. Above all, they have distinguished themselves as true gun-ships of great fire power which, by the very nature of their flight, are immensely flexible, ambling along as shotgun on a convoy one minute, the next a veritable high-speed killer, throwing bullets, grenades and rockets as it dives on the enemy—thus earning for itself the Viet Cong sobriquet of "muttering death".

Another unusual approach to this particular kind of warfare, and one which has achieved a worthwhile degree of success, has involved the use of specially-equipped aircraft to fly psychological missions. Their task was to fly over areas where the Viet Cong were known to be active, broadcasting and dropping leaflets inviting the recipients to throw away their arms and avail themselves of an amnesty and rehabilitation.

North of Saigon is the scene of the second war—one which has become known as the American War. For it is here where the majority of the American forces sent to Vietnam have been deployed—and where they have done most of the fighting and most of the dying—both on the ground and in the air. This is no cloak-and-dagger skirmish against isolated pockets of the Viet Cong, but full-scale battle against a well trained and equipped North Vietnamese Army.

Here, as in the Delta area to the south, FACs play a vital rôle, both in the air and on the ground, calling in Navy, Air Force and Marine striking power to the point where it is needed most and at the right moment. It is in this area too, in the main, that the McDonnell F-4 Phantoms of the Air Force's 48th Tactical Fighter Squadron have tangled with, and more often than not, bested the MiG-21s.

Nowhere has the work of reconnaissance aircraft been more valuable than in Vietnam and the 13th Reconnaissance Wing, based at Tan Son Nhut in the Delta area, could call upon RB-57 Canberras, RB-66 Destroyers, RF-101 Voodoos and RF-4C Phantoms, to carry out this exacting task by day or night.

So good was the work of this unit that, on occasion, low-altitude reconnaissance photographs have pinpointed guerilla bases by the tell-tale of such items as a single-stranded aerial wire, or a small pile of chopped firewood.

The RB-57 Canberra was, of course, another time-expired servant, but one that proved ideal for very-high-altitude coverage of large areas. Photographs taken at such altitude provide a good basis for overall comparison, and any slight change noted between one sortie and another was accorded closer investigation by low-flying Voodoos during daylight hours, or by the Phantoms at night. These latter aircraft could not only take photographs by conventional means, but also by infra-red and radar techniques, which meant there was little the enemy could hide from 13 Wing's prying eyes. Intelligent usage of the reconnaissance wing did much to limit US casualties, for by this medium it was possible to alert appropriate units whenever there were signs of a large-scale infiltration of enemy forces.

The third war, the Out-Country war as the Americans called it, dealt with this problem of supplies, reinforcements and large-scale infiltration: the Ho Chi Minh trail which was the main inward route was bombed constantly, as was North Vietnam, Laos, and the waterways and coastal routes leading to South Vietnam.

In World War II the USAF had realised the importance of interdiction and soon discovered that Vietnam was no exception to this rule. Once again, bridges proved to be the most difficult and costly targets for, vital to the enemy, great ingenuity was used to combat Air Force efforts to destroy them. One neat idea involved reconstruction of damaged bridges with the carriage surface just below the muddy water of the fast-flowing rivers, making it very difficult to detect them from the air. And to discourage the USAF from attacking them at all, they were defended by a veritable hail of vertical fire which included ack-ack, 20-mm cannon, mortar and small arms fire, together with masses of surface-to-air missiles, principally Russian-made SA-2 Guidelines. Being designed to cope with targets above 1,500 feet these missiles were not too troublesome in themselves, for it was of course possible to fly below their effective height. Unfortunately, this was a very suitable range for more conventional weapons, and consequently a large proportion of damage or destruction has been caused by weapons that might have been considered outdated.

Principal aircraft in this theatre were USAF F-105 Thunderchiefs and Marine F-4C Phantoms. Since both were based at long range from their targets—the Thunderchiefs in Thailand, the Phantoms at Danang—in-flight refuelling became routine on most operations, and it was common practice for KC-135 jet tankers to feed the fighters both before and after attack. Other hungry aircraft were the B-52s from Guam which, having carried some 50 750-lb bombs for nearly 2,500 miles, needed a satisfying drink from the tankers to provide adequate range for a safe return to their island home.

This is a fair example of how the USAF has adapted itself to new circumstances. In World War II, for example, flight refuelling had no part of combat operations. In Vietnam the demands upon the tanker fleet have grown steadily: they have become an important essential for this type of war. But there are few who would envy the crews of these aircraft their task, driving around an airborne petrol tanker in the midst of a shooting war.

Indeed, examples of great courage were evident for all to see. But the credit for sheer guts must go surely to the crews of the "Jolly Green Giants", the Sikorsky CH-3E helicopters, whose task was to rescue fighter crews down in the dense jungles of North Vietnam. Faced with long-range, low-altitude, slow-speed flight over miles of enemy territory, the experiences of these crews would provide a history of adventure second to none.

By the end of 1966, little more than eighteen months from the time when American manpower began to build up in Vietnam, it was clear that the US had become involved in what was likely to prove a costly war. Of even more concern was the fact that there seemed little hope of an early peace. In fact, was Kennedy's "any price" enough to prevent escalation of this conflict?

And in any case what is any price? How do you measure it? In terms of the billions of dollars spent on weapons, or the dreadful and seemingly endless sacrifice of the young, and not-so-young?

Some slight indication of the cost of this war is given by an estimated price tag of $100,000 for each member of the Viet Cong that have been killed by American arms.

As 1966 ended the majority of people in the West, not necessarily in America, would have agreed that "any price" had not been too high a figure to prevent expansion of this war in the Far East allowing, as it did, the rest of the world to live in comparative peace.

But there were those in America who were beginning to question, for the first time, whether "any price" was not far too costly a bill for the nation to bear, particularly in a war so remote from her own shores, and one that looked as if it might have no ending.

Veil of the Future

. . . Lift the veil of the future and show us the generation to come. . . .
Grant us a vision of the far-off years as they may be if redeemed by the
sons of God, that we may take heart and do battle for Thy children
and ours. . . .
Walter Rauschenbusch. Prayers of Social Awakening, 1910

IT IS FORTUNATE that the gaze of we mortals cannot, in the main, penetrate the veil of the future. There are, of course, many who express a desire for some pre-knowledge of their fates—provided that the predictions of those who earn their living by such means foretell only good news. There can be very few people, indeed, being granted details of the worst that the future might hold for them, who could accept the situation with philosophic calm.

Perhaps we may be excused our prejudice if we conjecture that an insight into the future might be desirable for those leaders who plan the defence of our "Western" civilisation: it could be very useful to make preparations to meet almost any eventuality, however dreadful.

Our leaders, though, are only human, and can but make reasoned and wise provision for whatever the future may hold. Their task is no enviable one, for who can possibly tell what entirely new weapons or revolutionary techniques may lie just around the corner. One needs only to look back at developments during the 1957—66 decade—at events which changed the face of the USAF—to appreciate the amazing speed of modern technological advance.

For the United States Air Force 1967 brought no brighter, happier future. They were still heavily committed in Vietnam, where a "conventional" war with "conventional" weapons was proving effective enough to kill far too many good men.

The pattern of war followed that of the three previous years, except that there was a steady increase in the number of men and weapons engaged, but as 1967 advanced Air Force activity was such that it began to force a change in the pattern of the ground fighting. With B-52s based on Thailand, as well as Guam, it became possible to increase the number of sorties flown by these aircraft. By mid-June 1967, they had dropped no less than 190,000 tons of bombs on Communist territory, and as the weight of this attack increased it became clear to the enemy that it was no longer possible for him to mass large concentrations of troops. In future, he would be restricted to the use of small units, of a size not likely to compel the attention of the Stratofortresses.

There was a major exception to this pattern in 1968, when the North Vietnamese general Vo Nguyen Giap decided to attack the key South Vietnamese base of Khe Sanh, situated at the western end of the Demilitarised Zone.

In late January, Giap was estimated to have a total force of some 200,000 men surrounding Khe Sanh, strategically situated on high ground where his artillery could dig in. Not only was Giap confident of success—as well he might be with a garrison of but 6,000 men opposing him, and one that was, to all intents and purposes, cut off from reinforcements and supplies—but he believed that a major victory at Khe Sanh would precipitate a situation in which the Americans might pull out of Vietnam for good.

Sadly, for him, he had not taken full account of the potential of air power. Starting on January 21, 1968, the USAF, aided by Naval and Marine aircraft, taught Giap a lesson he is unlikely to forget, hitting his North Vietnamese troops with 100,000 tons of bombs and some 700,000 rounds of cannon or machine-gun fire.

It was more than enough. By March 12 Giap ordered a major withdrawal. He had no alternative for the position of his troops was untenable: the unrelenting and almost continual barrage not only prevented him from obtaining reinforcements and supplies, but was literally decimating his force before his very eyes.

The USAF looks towards the future by equipping to deploy this type of massive conventional fire power almost immediately at any point on the world's surface, thus making possible a "fire-brigade" service to stamp out little wars before they have time to develop into big ones. To this end, Military Air Transport Service had fourteen squadrons of Lockheed C-141 Star Lifters in service by 1968, and aims to have six squadrons of the giant Lockheed C-5A Galaxy transports operational by 1972.

A practical demonstration of what such a force could do was given in 1967, when two brigades of the 101st Airborne Division, amounting to 10,000 troops and 5,300 tons of equipment, were airlifted from Kentucky to Vietnam. If the time factor had been critical the entire operation could have been completed in under a week.

To extend the ability of the Air Force to deal firmly with insurrection new counter-insurgency (COIN) and FAC aircraft are to join the ranks, and an aircraft known as an Advanced Manned Strategic Aircraft (AMSA) and now designated B-1 is being studied by the planning councils of the Defense Department. A manned interceptor of the future may well be developed from an aircraft like the YF-12A, while development of an air-superiority fighter for the USAF seems assured, as the McDonnell Douglas Corporation has been awarded a contract to produce an initial quantity of 107 Mach 2·5 delta-wing fighters, under the designation F-15.

Greatly improved battlefield mobility would be offered by the provision of a fighter which could take off and land vertically (VTOL). Such an aircraft would be able to operate without a need for prepared landing strips and, consequently, could be based close to the front line where it would be of the maximum value. Such an aircraft already exists in the British-built Hawker Siddeley Harrier, and USAF planners have already shown considerable interest in this revolutionary weapon, able to lift vertically out of a confined space and yet capable of supersonic flight. In this case, however, the USAF have already been forestalled by the US Marine Corps, which has placed orders now totalling 30 aircraft.

During the last year or so ordinary men and women throughout the world seem to have gained the opinion that the "cold war" has become a little less intense and that, in consequence, it should be possible to put less emphasis on nuclear deterrence. USAF leaders do not see it this way. They argue that the growing nuclear strength of the Soviet Union, and the growing nuclear potential of Communist China, compels the maintenance—so far as possible—of a margin of nuclear superiority.

A significant portion of this deterrent depends still upon Strategic Air Command's B-52s, which first entered service fourteen years ago. Their potential has been enhanced with the passage of time, for not only have improved models of the Stratofortress entered service, but evolution of the weapons and countermeasures that these aircraft can deploy means that it can continue to play a vital rôle in American strategy.

The other vital component of SAC's deterrent policy, the Minuteman ICBM, has grown in importance as it has become operational in greater numbers. By January 5, 1959, they totalled 1,000, including 350 Minuteman IIs, hidden from sight in their underground silos and ready for instant and massive retaliation.

Looking to the future, SAC already has the improved Minuteman III under construction and Minuteman IV on the drawing board, and to ensure that her ICBMs will not be eliminated by an enemy making the first strike, it is programmed for all of these weapons to be housed in superhard silos, making them safe from all but a direct hit.

References to SAC's missiles recalls the first of the ICBMs—Atlas—which was completely phased out of the strategic missile force by the end of 1965. Though no longer an operational weapon it had a valuable life ahead as a launch vehicle. It was Air Force Atlas boosters, each with an Agena upper stage, that put the Lunar Orbiter spacecraft in orbit around the Moon. These were equipped to photograph the Moon's surface and relay the pictures back to Earth. In a highly successful programme, which ended in August 1967, five Lunar Orbiters were launched and these, between them, succeeded in photographing almost 100 per cent of the Lunar surface.

Simultaneously, Atlas-Centaurs were launching Surveyor vehicles to soft-land on the Moon and the last of these, Surveyor 7, was launched on January 7, 1968. Their task was to survey possible landing sites for future astronauts, to discover whether the environment would prove hostile or friendly to man, and to ensure that the Moon's surface would support the weight of a landing craft. Though Surveyors 2 and 4 crashed into the Moon, the remainder performed very much as planned, providing the basic data required of them as well as being vehicles for a number of other scientific experiments.

In fact, the stage was being set for man's first great voyage into space for on November 9, 1967, before the last Surveyor had set out on its voyage of discovery, the gigantic Saturn V three-stage launch vehicle, over 353 feet in height and weighing 6,100,000 lb at take-off (over 2,723 tons) had placed the unmanned Apollo 4 spacecraft into Earth orbit.

Due to a tragic accident on January 27, 1967, when during ground tests of Spacecraft 012 astronauts Roger Chaffee, Virgil Grissom and Edward White lost their lives, there was considerable delay before a manned Apollo flight. When Apollo 7 was launched with a three-man crew on October 11, 1968, it was the first United States manned space flight since the last of the two-man Gemini capsules had splashed down in 1966.

Moon overture was heard by millions as Saturn's Rocketdyne engines thundered on December 21, 1968, lifting Apollo 8 towards the Moon, providing a never-to-be-forgotten Christmas for men, women and children throughout the world who, by the medium of television, watched with breathless wonder as Apollo cruised some 70 miles above the Moon's surface.

Apollo 10, launched on May 18, 1969, was the dress rehearsal for Moon landing, and once again the world thrilled as the Lunar Module *Snoopy* approached within 9 miles of the ultimate target.

Finally, on Wednesday, July 16, 1969, Apollo 11 blasted off the launch pad at Cape Kennedy *en route* to the Moon. On board were Neil Armstrong (Commander), Edwin Aldrin (Lunar Module pilot) and Michael Collins (Command Module pilot).

At 21 hours 6 minutes BST on Sunday, July 21, the Lunar Module *Eagle*, carrying Armstrong and Aldrin, was at the "high gate", 50,000 feet above the Moon's surface. A television camera looking out of *Eagle* allowed the world to peer over the astronauts' shoulders as their frail-looking craft journeyed down to the desolate landscape below.

Twelve minutes later, in a flurry of lunar dust, *Eagle* settled on the Moon and a breathless audience heard the words: "Contact lights. O.K., engines stop. Tranquility Base here. The *Eagle* has landed."

Thus, at 21 hours 17 minutes 42 seconds BST on July 21, 1969, man had overcome seemingly impossible technicalities to land safely on the Moon some quarter of a million miles away. Of the two astronauts to land, one was an officer of the United States Air Force—Col. Edwin "Buzz" Aldrin.

A historic event for the world and a moment of great pride for the USAF. In the brief span of just under sixty years, beginning with the shaky solo flights of Lt. Lahm and Lt. Humphreys in Signal Corps aircraft No. 1, America's air arm had reached out into space.

Whatever may lay hidden behind the veil of the future, there seems little doubt that America's air force will endeavour to remain abreast of events. But it should not be forgotten that the 200,000-strong US Air Service which had seen the end of World War I, was quickly decimated to an ineffectual 10,000 men with obsolete aircraft. The mighty USAAF which, with its Allies, had shown the world the capability of air power during World War II, soon dwindled to a shadow of its former self after the defeat of Japan. Let us hope that, once again, history will not repeat itself and that the USAF which has done, and continues to do, so much to inhibit Communist expansion, will not be rendered impotent by the economic demands of the moment.

Given the essential finance, advanced technology and preparedness will mean that those men and women who proudly bear the emblem of the USAF on their uniforms, will continue to do their utmost to ensure that the immortal words of Abraham Lincoln will prevail:

". . . that government of the people, by the people, for the people, shall not perish from the earth."

First balloon ascent in the US was made by Jean-Pierre Blanchard from Philadelphia in 1793—but there was no military ballooning until the Civil War. Here, during the battle of Fair Oaks, members of the Union army inflate the balloon *Intrepid*

On December 17, 1903, powered flight became reality when the Wright brothers' *Flyer* left the ground for the first time, covering a distance of 120ft

The balloon section of the US Army's Signals Corps was formed in 1892: its single balloon was lost at the Battle of San Juan Hill in the Spanish-American War. Not until the Aeronautical Division was established, on August 1, 1907, were ballooning activities resumed, pending receipt of heavier-than-air craft. At Fort Meyer, Virginia, in the early summer of 1908, we see the Signal Corps preparing a balloon for flight

Military balloons were intended for observation and control of artillery fire, and the Signals Corps were quick to rehearse the deployment of their captive balloons and to experiment with photography and communications

Captive balloons had but limited reconnaissance value: free balloons were at the beck and call of every breeze. A powered balloon—or airship—seemed to offer the best solution to the problem and in the summer of 1908 the Signals Corps accepted a dirigible airship which it flew at Fort Meyer

Orville Wright demonstrating the Wright Type A at Fort Meyer in
August 1908. This is the aircraft in which Lt. Thomas E. Selfridge was
injured fatally on September 17, 1908

Earlier in that same summer, on July 4, Glenn H. Curtiss had made a first flight in his *June Bug*—a more practical-looking aeroplane than the Wright *Flyer*. It was a Curtiss Model D that became the Army's second official aeroplane

"Aeroplane No. 1, Heavier-than-air Division, United States aerial Fleet", was how the Washington *Evening Star* dubbed this Wright Type B, accepted by the Signals Corps on August 2, 1909. Note the ground handling wheels

The Wright Type B at Fort Meyer later in 1909, after it had been equipped with landing wheels. Posing in this photograph are Lt. Benjamin D. Foulois (fourth from left) and the entire strength of the Signal Corps' Aeronautical Division

Lt. Roy Kirtland at the controls of a Wright Type B at College Park, Maryland, in 1911, following the return from Fort Sam Houston, Texas

That the Signals Corp was unprepared to accept only a passive
reconnaissance rôle was demonstrated as early as January
1911. Phillip O. Parmalee and Lt. M. S. Crissy in a Wright
machine at San Francisco, California, prepare to drop the
Air Corp's first ''bomb''

Capt. Charles de F. Chandler
(left) and Lt. Roy T. Kirtland
helped to advance thoughts on
combat aircraft when, on June
7, 1912, they fired a Lewis
machine-gun from a Wright
Type B

Limited range meant it was desirable that aircraft could be
carried by surface transport close to where they would be
deployed. A Wright Type C is dismantled for carriage by
rail in October 1912

An aviation section was formed at Fort McKinley in the
Philippine Islands in February 1912, with Lt. Frank Lahm in
command. He is shown standing third from left, with a
Wright Type C as background

Lt. Herbert A. Dargue standing by his damaged Curtiss JN-3
aircraft at Chihuahua City, Mexico, in 1916. This punitive
expedition into Mexico was the Signal Corp's first "warlike"
mission

With the US involved in the
first World War, balloons
again became important, particularly for observation. This
kite balloon is typical of those
employed on the Mexican
border in 1917

The US Air Service pilots were, in the main, trained in Europe. Here
Americans are seen in training at a French flying school at Tours in 1918.
The rather flimsy French-built Morane trainers bore little resemblance
to the combat aircraft they would fly at the front

A French-built Spad single-seat fighter of the 94th Pursuit Squadron,
the famous "Hat-in-the-Ring" squadron

Capt. Eddie Rickenbacker, the Air Service's top fighter ace who was credited with destroying 26 enemy aircraft, poses in front of a Spad fighter

General Benjamin D. Foulois at Colombey-les-Belles, France, in 1918. When the Air Service came to France in 1917 he had been Chief of the Air Service, AEF

The British-designed de Havilland 4 was
one of several British and French designs
considered for construction in America.
The DH-4 was the only one produced in
any quantity, and following detail re-
design was known as the Liberty Plane.
General Foulois poses in front of one of
the aircraft at Colombey-les-Belles, July
28, 1918

Most extensively-built American aircraft
of World War I were the Curtiss Jennies,
a name derived from the official JN
designation. The Army evaluated its first
JN in 1914 and the last of these machines
were withdrawn from service in 1927.
War-surplus Jennies supplied a generation of postwar barnstormers and private
flyers

In the spring of 1918 Curtiss developed a two-seat fighter powered by a 400hp Kukham K-12 engine. Biplane (Model 18-B Hornet) and triplane (Model 18-T Wasp) versions were produced and the 18-T, seen here, held the world speed record at 163mph for some time

Despite indifferent equipment, Air Service personnel lost little time in demonstrating the pioneering spirit. A Martin MB-2, powered by two 420hp Liberty engines, set out in November 1919 with two pilots and two mechanics to circumnavigate the United States

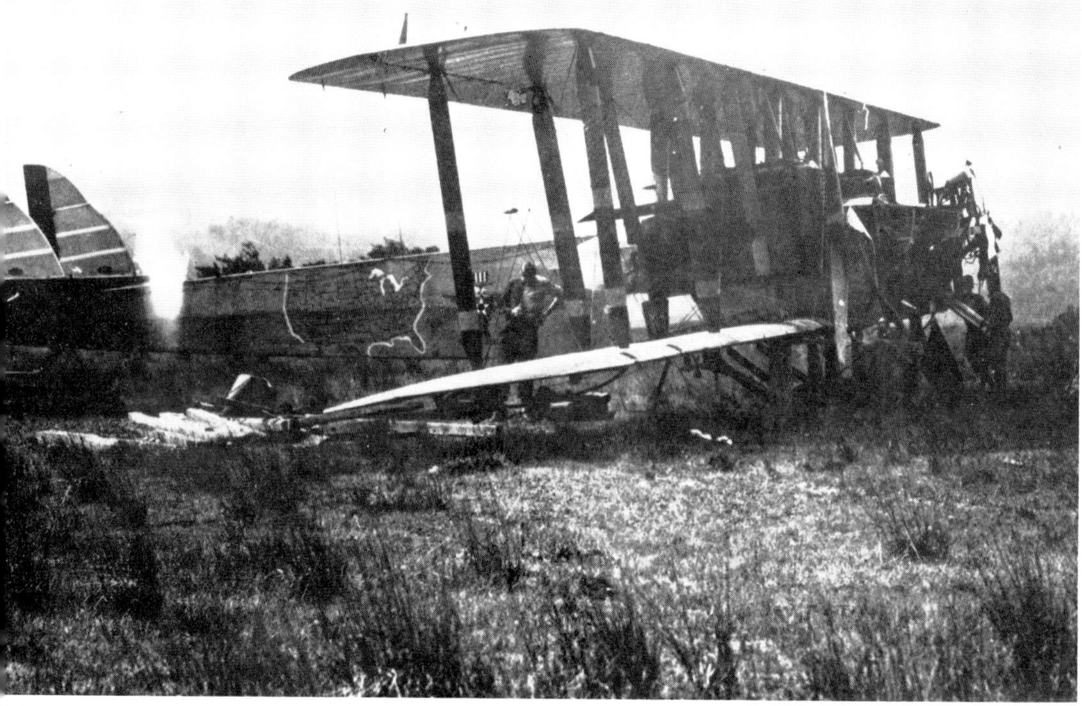

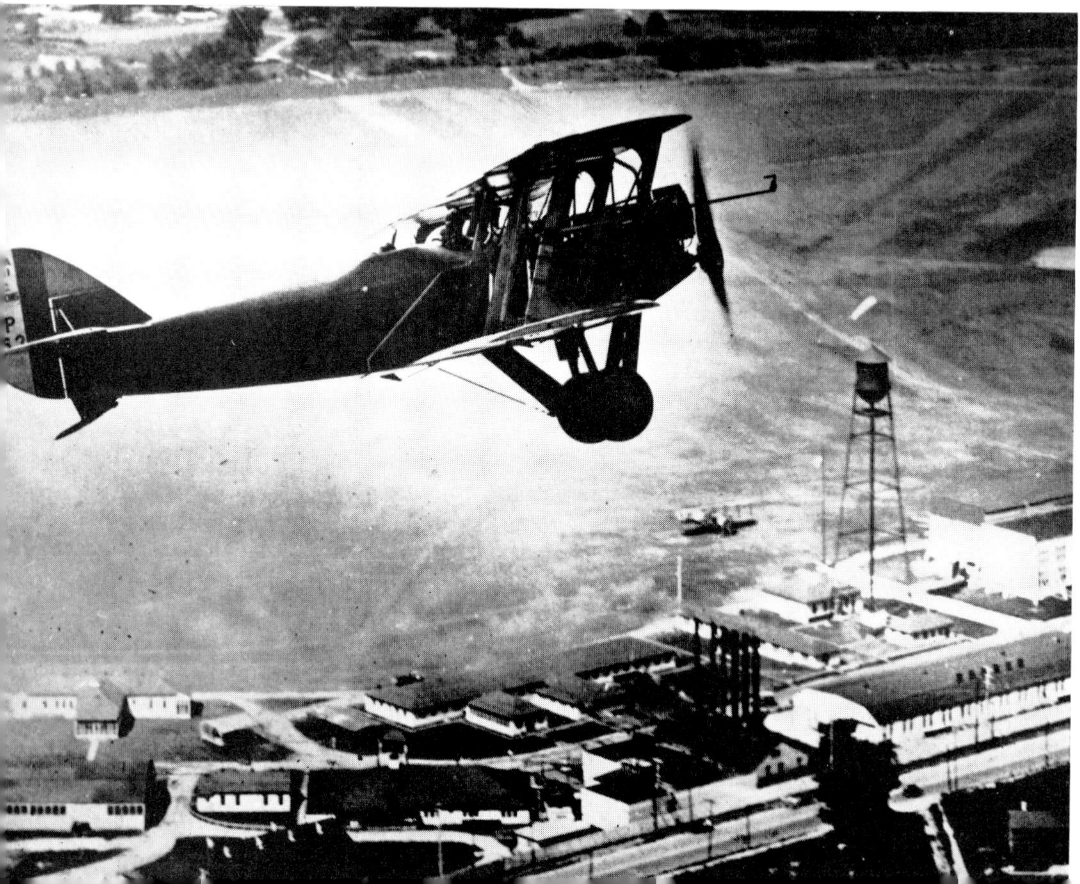

A Martin NBS-1 (Night Bomber, Short-range) taking off in 1920. This was the US Army's only specially-designated night bomber

This photograph of the MB-2 during its ''round-the-rim'' flight would indicate a nose-in. Nevertheless, aircraft and crew completed successfully the 9,823-mile flight

Seen over McCook Field in 1919, a Packard-Le Pere LUSAC-11, powered by a 400hp Liberty engine. Major Rudolph W. Schroeder and Lt. G. E. Elfrey used the aircraft to attain a world record altitude of 31,821ft on October 4, 1919. A little more than four months later, on February 27, 1920, Maj. Schroeder achieved a solo altitude record of 33,113ft

Brigadier Gen. ''Billy'' Mitchell, Assistant-Chief of the Air Service, photographed by a Lewis & Vought VE-7 advanced trainer in May 1920. Only small numbers of the VE-7 were produced, as the demand for this type of aircraft was met by converting Curtiss JN-4s to Hispano-powered JN-4Hs

One of Mitchell's first carefully-planned demonstrations to show the potential of air power was a New York to Nome, Alaska, return flight by four DH-4Bs, led by Capt. St Clair Street. Here, on October 27, 1920, Gen. John J. Pershing (right) congratulates Capt. Street on the completion of his mission

Most spectacular of Mitchell's demonstrations were the attacks made by Martin MB-2 bombers on German and US battleships at anchor. Here the USS *Alabama* is neatly bracketed by a phosphorus bomb

A happy photograph of Billy Mitchell, seated at the controls of a Curtiss PW-8, forerunner of the famous line of Curtiss Hawks. Little over two years later a court-martial suspended Mitchell from duty

One of the early "big bombers" was this single XNBL-1 "Barling Bomber", designed by Walter Barling of the Engineering Division and built by the Witteman-Lewis Company of Teterboro, New Jersey. Underpowered, slow and unable to climb over the Appalachians, it was scrapped in 1928

The four specially-built Douglas DWCs (Douglas World Cruisers) before the start of the epic flight on April 6, 1924. Two DWCs still exist as museum pieces: one at the Smithsonian Institute, the other in the Air Force Museum at Wright-Patterson AFB

A poor quality but historic picture of one of the Douglas DWCs in the air near Seattle, Washington, just before the start of the world flight attempt

The Royal Navy gives a hand to refuel the Douglas World Cruiser *New Orleans* at Houton Bay in the Orkney Islands, Scotland

Rare bird of the mid 'twenties was this one and only Engineering Division XCO-5, a variant of the TP-1, and which Lt. John A. Macready used to gain an American altitude record of 38,704ft on January 29, 1926

Lt. "Jimmy" Doolittle with the Curtiss R3C-2 after winning the 1925 Schneider Cup for the USA at Baltimore on October 26. Two weeks earlier the same aircraft, with wheeled undercarriage and designated R3C-1, had carried Lt. Cy Bettis to victory in the 1925 Pulitzer Trophy Race

Lt. H. H. Mills photographed with the R3 after winning the 1924 Pulitzer Trophy Race. Designed by Alfred Verville of the Engineering Division and built by the Sperry Aircraft Company, the R3 was powered by a 500hp Curtiss D-12 engine. Note early retractable undercarriage

The DH-4 served the air force well for almost 13 years. Truly ubiquitous, its duties ranged from aerial ambulance to target-tug; trainer to gas barrage layer. Illustrated is a photo-reconnaissance version

Four of 15 OA-1 amphibians, built by the Loening Aeronautical Engineering Corporation, were used by the Air Service for a 22,605-mil geoodwill tour of Central and South America

As late as 1925 the Air Services could still demonstrate lighter-than-air techniques: a jumping-balloon taking part in an International Air Race

Loening OA-1 *New York*, flagship of the Pan American flight and flown by the leader of the expedition, Maj. Herbert A. Dargue, comes ashore at Fort de France Bay, Martinique

The refuelling technique was practised again and again before the record attempt. A Douglas C-1 combined cargo/personnel transport serves as the flight tanker

The Air Service had pioneered flight refuelling on June 27, 1923. This technique was to be used in an endurance record attempt early in 1929. Here, the Fokker F-VIIA/3m, Air Service designation C-2A, but best known as the *Question Mark*, is seen during trials in December 1928

Between January 1–7, 1929, the *Question Mark*, commanded by Maj. Carl Spaatz, remained airborne for almost 151 hours. This picture shows flight refuelling in progress over Burbank, California, during the record attempt

The tired but elated crew of the *Question Mark*: left to right, Sgt. Roy Hooe, Lt. Elwood Quesada, Lt. Harry Halverson, Capt. Ira C. Baker and Maj. Carl Spaatz

Curtiss P-6E Hawks lined up at Air Corps headquarters in the early 1930s. The P-1 Hawk had been the first to carry the P for pursuit designation

Keen to prove that its new B-10 bombers could
reinforce outlying bases, Lt. Col. "Hap" Arnold
(left) and Maj. Ralph Royce study the route of
the planned ten-bomber flight to Alaska

Lt. Col. Arnold receives the key to the city of
Fairbanks, in appreciation of the Air Corp's
achievement

The Martin B-10s lined up at Fairbanks, Alaska,
after an uneventful flight

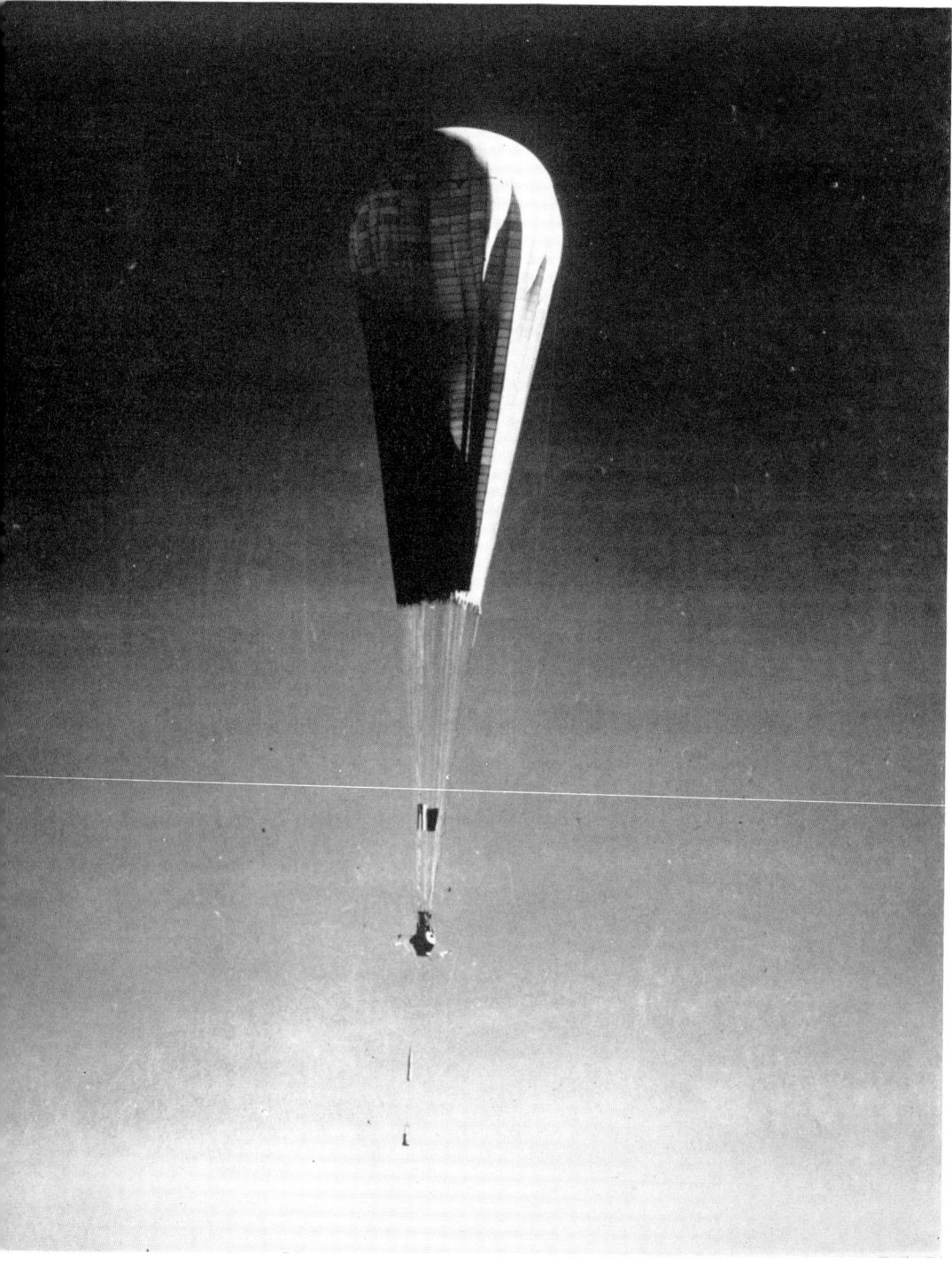

Even in the mid-1930s balloons could still perform useful service. On July 28, 1934, the Air Corps/National Geographic Society balloon *Explorer* carried Maj. W. E. Kepner and Capts. A. W. Stevens and O. A. Anderson to a height of 60,613ft

A line of Boeing-built DH-4Ms is drawn up for general inspection in the summer of 1928

First all-metal monoplane fighter aircraft of the
Air Corps, the Boeing P-26 served with many
pursuit squadrons. When the Air Corps
ordered 136 P-26As in 1933, it represented the
largest single contract placed for eleven years

A neatly stacked formation of Boeing P-26As.
Maximum speed of these fighters was about
230mph and armament comprised two fixed
forward-firing 0·30in machine-guns: a 112lb
bomb load could be carried on external racks

In 1939 the Douglas B-18 was the principal weapon of the Air Corps. Developed from the DC-2 commercial transport, it had a maximum speed of 215mph at 10,000ft

The *Explorer II* Air Corps/NGS research balloon seen near Rapid City, South Dakota, shortly before Capt. A. W. Stevens and O. A. Anderson attained a new record altitude of 72,394ft on November 9, 1935

The other major component of the 1939 Air Corps was the Northrop A-17A, a 220mph fighter armed with five machine-guns

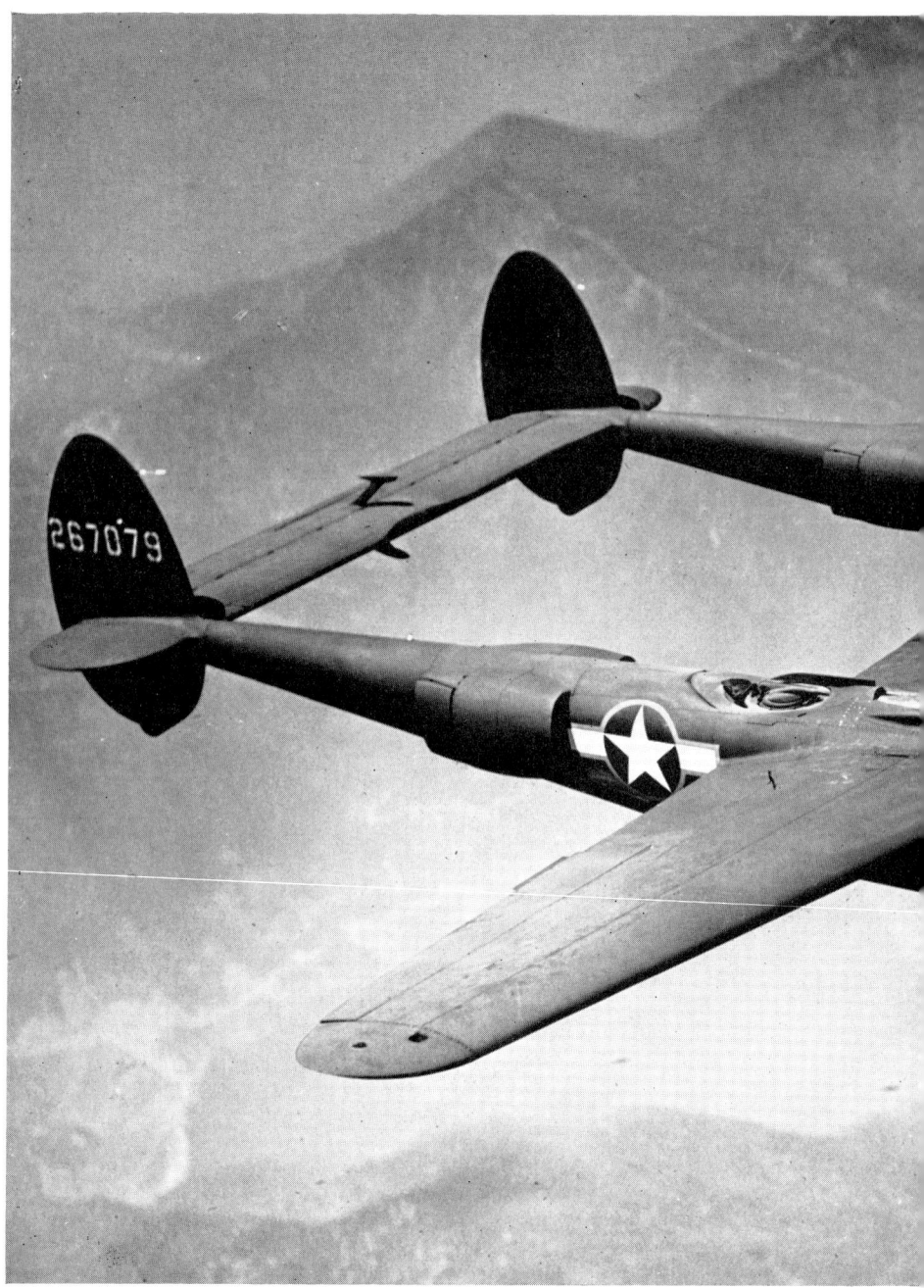

The P-38 Lightning was the Lockheed Company's first military project. Lockheed chose a twin-engined layout to meet a 1937 specification, and the company's revolutionary twin-boom fighter was heavier than many contemporary bombers. This P-38G of 1943 had a top speed of almost 400mph

War in Europe spurred the American aircraft industry to produce more modern weapons. One of the first to enter service was the Bell P-39 Airacobra, its engine buried in the fuselage behind the pilot. Armament comprised a 37mm or 25mm nose-mounted cannon

The "Attack" category was represented by the Douglas Havoc. The example shown here is an A-20G with electrically-powered dorsal turret

Following the armament pattern of contemporary British fighters, this Republic P-47D Thunderbolt had eight 0·50in wing-mounted machine-guns

The B-18s were soon ousted by a new family of bombers. The Martin B-26 Marauder was a 300mph twin-engined medium bomber

The aircraft that commemorated the name of "Billy" Mitchell, the North American B-25 Mitchell, first of which entered service with the 17th Bombardment Group at McChord Field in 1941

The four-engined Consolidated B-24 Liberator was built in greater quantity than any other American aircraft of World War II, and could carry more than 8,000lb of bombs

Best-known of the USAAF's wartime bombers was the Boeing B-17 Flying Fortress. This B-17E had a range of 2,400 miles with a 4,000lb bomb load, or could carry a maximum 17,600lb load over shorter range

The success of German Ju 87 dive-bombers interested the Air Corps sufficiently for them to order the Douglas A-24 attack bomber, a modified version of the US Navy's Douglas SBD

On April 18, 1942, little more than four months from the Japanese attack on Pearl Harbor, Lt. Col. "Jimmy" Doolittle led the famed "Doolittle Raid" on Tokyo. Here a B-25 Mitchell is seen taking off for this attack from the carrier USS *Hornet*

B-17s of the 8th Air Force spearheaded the USAAF's daylight attack on Germany. The smoke trails are from markers dropped by earlier aircraft

This B-17 limped home and landed safely after a Nazi fighter had crashed into it over Germany

Bombs fall from the Fortresses during an attack on Bremen in 1943

Typical of the wartime sky over Europe, Fortresses streaming contrails

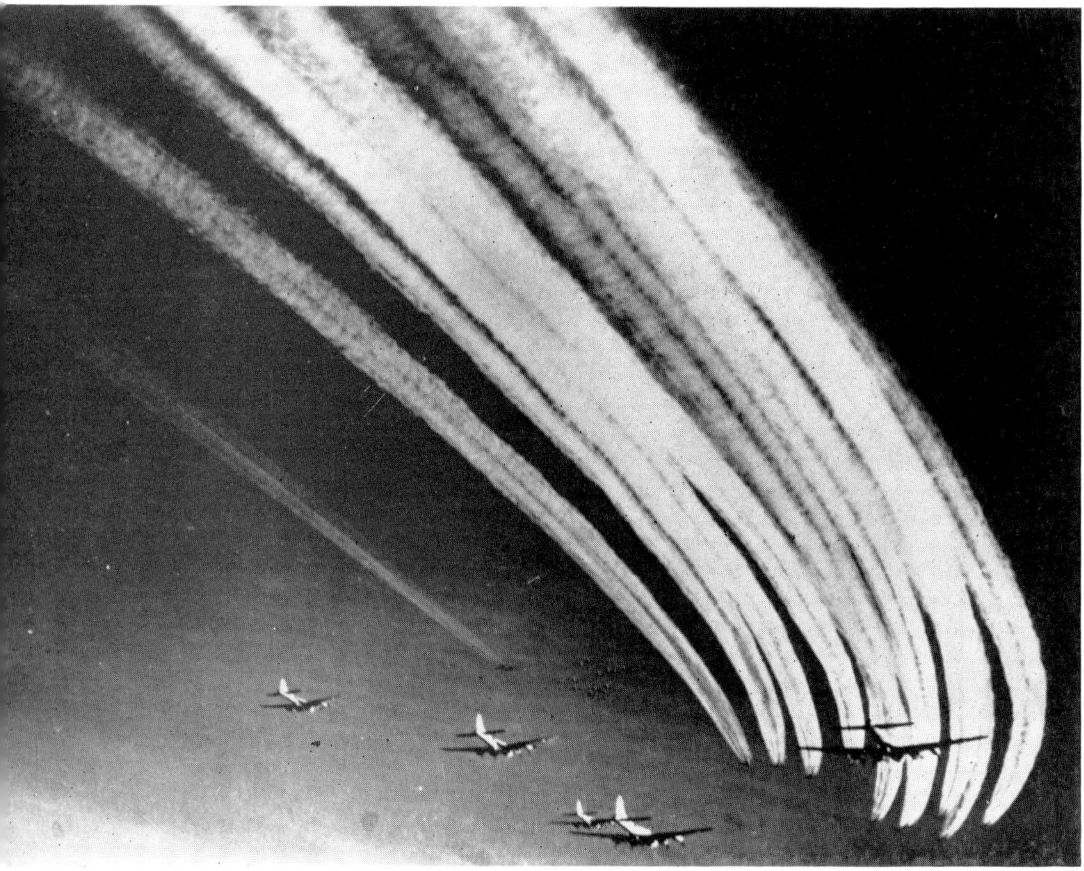

Sticks of bombs falling from B-17s as German flak bursts at close quarters

Fortress hit by flak is engulfed in flames as the starboard wing breaks
away: none of her crew escaped

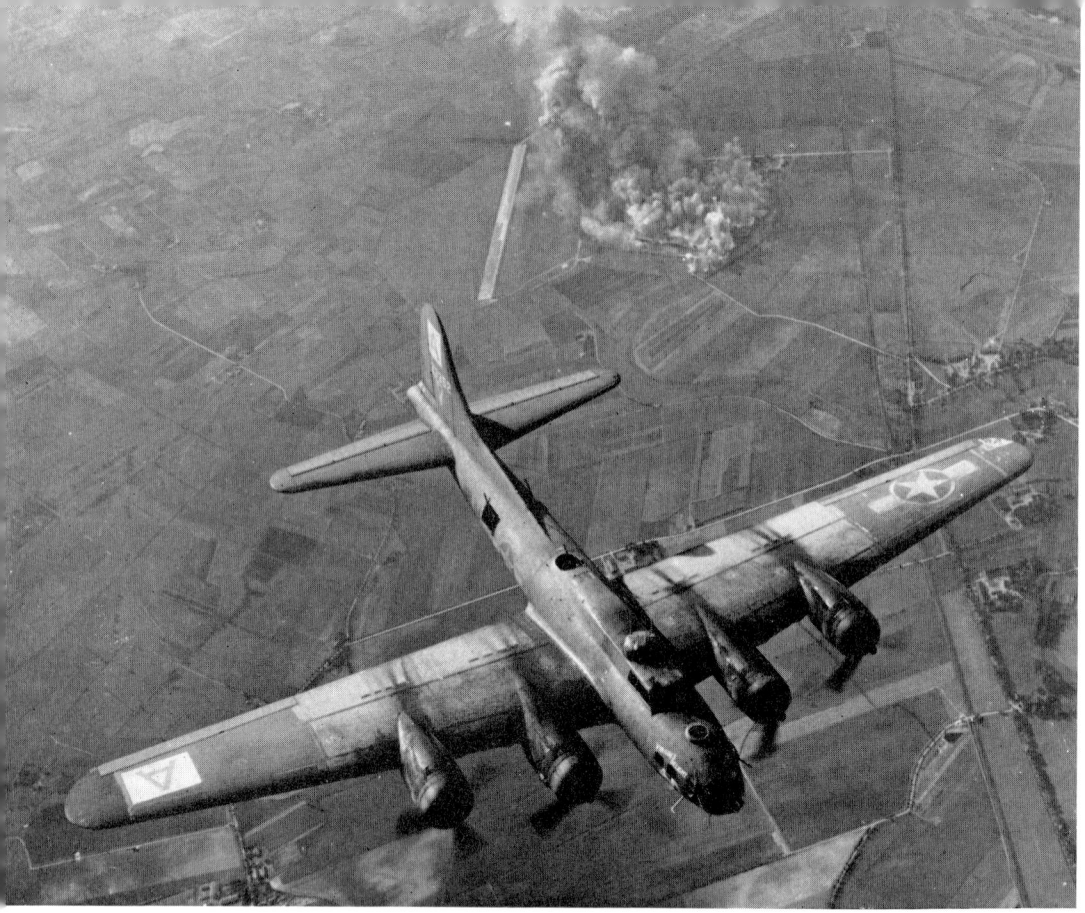

The precision of the USAAF's daylight bombing is well illustrated as a German airfield near Marienburg is bracketed by explosions

The shot gives a vivid impression of the conditions facing the B-24 Liberators that attacked the Ploesti refinery

Wreathed in flames is one of the Liberators that did not get back

The ubiquitous C-47 (commercial DC-3) of Air Transport Command
carries supplies over the Egyptian pyramids

The pilot of this 9th AAF P-47 Thunderbolt crash-landed and escaped
uninjured seconds before his aircraft burst into flames

The pilot of this Thunderbolt got away with it too, his aircraft streaking through the flaming debris of a German ammunition truck

A P-47 is taxied to its dispersal point in France, guided by a member of the ground crew riding on the port wing

B-26 Marauders of the 9th AAF hit at railway marshalling yards at Namur, Belgium

This Marauder loses an engine after a direct hit from an 88mm gun over France, crashing seconds later

The Marauders were a vital component of the 9th AAF, able to carry
up to 4,000lb bombs at around 300mph

One of the great fighters of World War II, the North American P-51 Mustang, made it possible to provide long-range fighter escort for the bombers that ranged the enemy sky by day

In preparation for the invasion of France, gliders and glider-towing techniques were explored to the full. This Curtiss C-46 Commando has a Waco CG-15A Hadrian 15/16-seat glider in tow

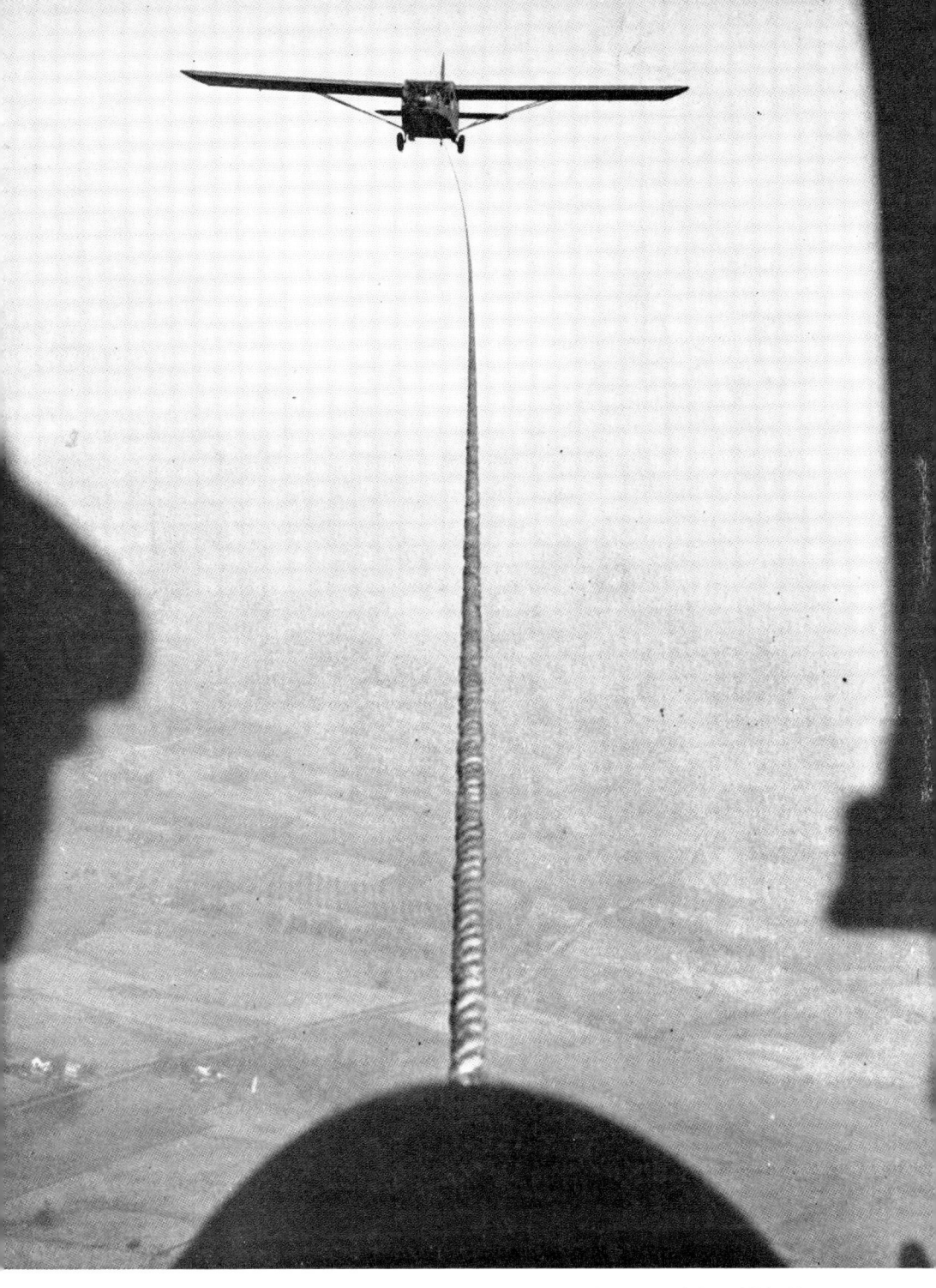

Unusual view of a Waco YCG-13, biggest American glider of World War II

By D-day, huge fleets of tugs and gliders were ready to drop troops at strategic points. Here two Douglas C-47s lead their charges across the Normandy coastline

A formation of Mustangs of the 375th Fighter Squadron, 361st Fighter Group, based in Great Britain

Judging by the mission records painted on this B-26 Marauder of the 554th Bomb Squadron, 386th Bomb Group, it was appropriately named

Its record was beaten by *Bar Fly*, a B-26 of the 9th AAF that eventually crashed on take-off after completing 175 missions

The B-26 was a superb tool for tactical and support duties. Here a 9th AAF Marauder turns for home, leaving the railway yards at Armentieres, France, with columns of smoke to serve as visiting card

French civilian workers patch up the runway of a former *Luftwaffe* airfield in France

B-26 Marauders of the 323rd Bomb Group line up ready for take-off at a snow-covered French airfield

Heavy flak greets Marauders attacking ground installations at Dieppe. The leading aircraft was seriously damaged, its bombardier killed and other crew members injured

The Nazi-held Schiphol Aerodrome at Amsterdam was attacked
regularly by the 9th AAF

Much of the Allied effort was concerned with destroying the German transport system. Marauders hit the bulls-eye at Haslach, Germany—

—while here a repair centre for German front-line motor transport is seen carpeted with bombs

The Cherbourg Peninsula, one of the last sectors to surrender to American forces, was given regular attention by the 9th AAF

Unusual low-level employment of a B-26 Marauder against a German factory: burst of fire from the nose-gun can be seen among the trees

To increase the speed of the Marauders they were stripped of camouflage paint. A brightly-polished formation leaves England *en route* for France

Strange-looking aircraft is, in fact, two Douglas A-26 Invaders attacking Germany's Siegfried Line

Close-support attacks against enemy strong points were often very costly; this flaming Marauder was hit by heavily-concentrated ack-ack

Lockheed P-38 Lightnings of the 15th AAF in formation over Yugoslavia

In the Pacific war, aircraft of a different era still had a part to play. This Curtiss Hawk of 1927 vintage carries forces' mail in Upper Assam in 1944

A Curtiss C-46 Commando takes the "hump" route to China

At the other end of the 500-mile ''hump'' route a C-46 touches down. Here, at Kunming, were found Chennault's Flying Tigers

Brig. Gen. C. Lee Chennault, who headed the newly-formed China Air Task Force in 1942, and later became the commander of the 14th AAF

Chennault had the drive to forge a mere handful of pilots and near obsolete aircraft into a most effective fighting unit. There was no lack of enthusiasm from these pilots scrambling to their P-40s

The 14th AAF fought at the end of the world's longest supply line, relying upon skilled American mechanics and some Chinese help to maintain a variety of aircraft that would have been scrapped in other combat areas

Open-air maintenance didn't help, neither did a more than hazardous supply of spares

This P-40 Tomahawk seems to have a mouthful of the Zero fighter it attacked and destroyed

Rare photograph of Col Jacob Smart welcoming Lt. Gen. Henry ''Hap'' Arnold to China in the dark days of 1943

Another rare photograph, taken early in 1943, links (left to right) Lt. Gen. ''Hap'' Arnold, Brig. Gen. Lee Chennault, General Joseph (''Vinegar Joe'') Stilwell, Sir John Dill and Brig. Gen. Clayton L. Bissell

The tiger-shark teeth painted on the P-40s soon earned the name "Flying Tigers". It became official when Maj. Gen. Lee Chennault accepted the first Tiger patch from its designers

There was no formal training for the Chinese, but they learnt quickly practical jobs such as gun cleaning and re-arming

Sturdy construction of the P-40 Tomahawk enabled it to gain its Chinese base after being hit by flak

Maintenance for the 14th AAF went on under most primitive conditions, while a Chinese soldier stands guard

In the later stages of the Pacific War, P-51 Mustangs began to appear in China. Those equipped to fire high-velocity aerial rockets were invaluable for ''loco-busting'' sweeps

Another reinforcement for the 14th AAF was the B-24: they averaged a superb 800 tons of shipping sunk per bombing sortie

Lt. Richard Bong, in the cockpit of his P-38 Lightning in New Guinea. With 40 enemy aircraft destroyed he became America's all-time ace

Curtiss P-40 Warhawks operated in every theatre of war. "Sue" of the 51st Fighter Group was based in India

It was as well that this Engineer Battalion "traffic cop" on the Mariannas did not order the P-47 Thunderbolts to halt

Maj. Gen. Ord Wingate, famous British commander, is carried by an aircraft of 1st Air Commando Force over Burma

B-25 Mitchells lay a smoke screen in the Southwest Pacific to hide troop movements

The Sikorsky R-4 was the first practical helicopter employed by the US armed forces. This YR-4B was tested under the tropical conditions of Burma

Cause and effect. A B-25 of the 345th Bomb Group attacks a Japanese frigate off the Chinese coast . . . with spectacular results . . . and a successful conclusion

Consolidated B-24 Liberators made their most significant contribution in the Pacific area. "Bolivar Jr" is seen over the Mariannas in 1945

Northrop P-61B Black Widow night fighters operating from the Marianna Islands and equipped with AI radar in the fuselage nose

The P-51 Mustang was no less valuable in the Pacific. These aircraft of the 1st Air Commando Force are patrolling over the Chin Hills, Burma

P-38M night fighter versions of the Lightning appeared in the Pacific area in the late stages of the war

The Boeing B-29 Superfortress enabled Gen. Curtis Le May to decimate Japan's major cities with low-level incendiary attacks by night. This B-29, "Enola Gay" carried an even more devastating weapon—

—the "Little Boy" nuclear bomb of the type detonated over Hiroshima, Japan, on August 6, 1945

Crew of the "Enola Gay", the captain, Col. Paul W. Tibbets, second from left

Nuclear bomb "Fat Boy" which was dropped on the naval port of Nagasaki by the B-29 "Bock's Car" on August 9, 1945

Development of nuclear weapons continued after the end of the Pacific War. This dramatic picture shows an underwater atomic explosion in the Pacific Ocean

At the base of this towering column of smoke lies the ruins of Nagasaki. Five days after this nuclear explosion the Japanese surrendered

Even more spectacular is this explosion at Bikini Atoll on July 25, 1946

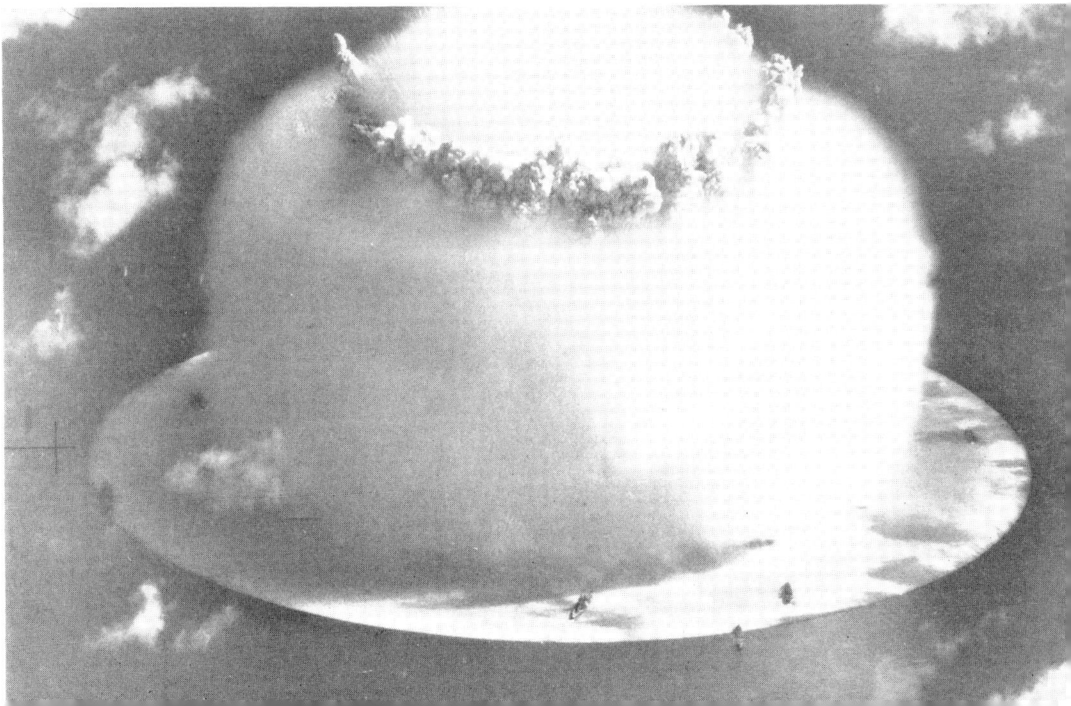

Inevitably, a postwar air force turned to exercises, like this "Operation Combine", in which Fairchild C-82 Packets spill out their loads of paratroops

The youthful USAF soon found itself involved in a man-size task—the Berlin Airlift. Here an aircraft follows the high-intensity approach lights to Tempelhof Airport, Berlin

The go-anywhere do-anything C-47s line up for unloading at Tempelhof
in what became known as "Operation Vittles"

Day and night the Berlin Airlift continued—posing complicated air
traffic control problems

Finally, on September 30, 1949, the last "Vittles" flight left Rhein Main Air Base

Close upon the heels of the Berlin Airlift came the Korean War. This F-82G Twin-Mustang fighter takes off from an advanced Far East Air Force base in Japan

At a critical period in the Korean War the North American F-86 Sabre
Jet fighter became operational

The "chopper" soon demonstrated its value in Korea.   This Sikorsky
H-19 Chickasaw demonstrates the technique that rescued pilots downed
behind enemy lines

Rapid airlift of injured men reduced battle fatalities to an all-time low
level. This Bell H-13 Sioux carries a wounded man to a modern
hospital in Southern Japan

An H-19 Chickasaw makes a simulated rescue over the Han River, near
Seoul

Psychologically important cargo—mail for the troops—is being loaded on board a "chopper" for delivery in forward areas

Combined rescue operations like this saved countless lives. A short-range Sikorsky H-5 rendezvous with an SA-16 Albatross amphibian, which will carry men to a rear area hospital

Unusual photograph shows four major combat aircraft of the Korean War. Top left an F-82 Twin Mustang, to its left an F-80 Shooting Star, on its right an F-94 Starfire all-weather fighter developed from the F-80 and at the bottom of the picture, an F-86 Sabre Jet

An F-80 Shooting Star takes off to strafe enemy lines in Korea

Republic F-84 Thunderjet which gave valuable service on interdiction sorties in Korea, and was also the aircraft in which flight refuelling techniques for jet-fighters was developed

The F-84 Thunderjet was able to deploy a wide range of weapons, and carried 1,800 rounds of 0·50in ammunition as well as bombs and rockets

The long-range B-29 Superfortress also had an important part to play in Korea—here military targets at Rashin are straddled by bombs

In Korea, as in all other theatres, transport was vital. Here a Fairchild C-119 Boxcar lands ahead of two F-80s

The first "giant" Douglas C-124 Globemaster arrives at a Korean airstrip carrying 11 tons of freight and 14 passengers. It was able to airlift about 74,000lb of cargo or 200 troops

Even trainer aircraft had a part to play in Korea. These North American T-6s were used to spot targets and direct the heavily-gunned fighters in to attack

War in Korea had shown the need for more potent fighters, leading to the "Century series". The X-series of research aircraft had been paving the way to this new generation. Here Maj. Charles "Chuck" Yeager congratulates Maj. Arthur Murray. In the X-1A, Yeager had travelled at 1,650mph, Murray attained an altitude of 90,000ft

And the Bell X-2 had flown at a reported 2,178mph

Convair's F-102 Delta Dagger all-w
century series, could climb as fast as

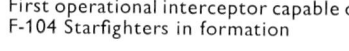

First of the Century series, the North American F-100 Super
Sabre was the world's first operational fighter capable of
supersonic speed in level flight

First operational interceptor capable c
F-104 Starfighters in formation

The McDonnell Aircraft Company's F-101 Voodoo fighter had
a then-phenomenal range of up to 2,800 miles and a maximum
speed of over 1,200mph

Republic's F-105 Thunderchief, able t
a maximum speed in excess of 1,400n

interceptor, third of the supersonic
d travel in level flight

Development at this period was looking in many directions.
This B-36D "mother" 'plane was equipped to launch and
retrieve a fast reconnaissance aircraft

ined speeds above Mach 2, Lockheed's

In fact, the 230ft-span RB-36D was the biggest aeroplane ever
to see service with the USAF, having six engines with pusher
propellers and four turbojets carried on underwing pods

14,000lb of external stores and with

Heavy strategic freighter, the Douglas C-133 Cargomaster,
could carry 200 troops and had a 13,000cu ft freight hold

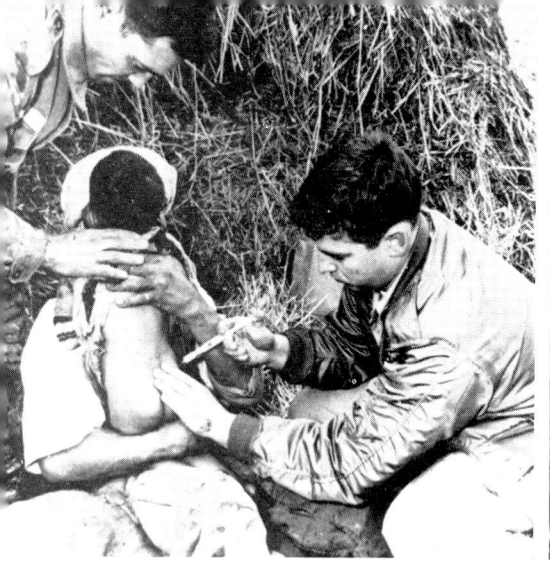

Aircraft like the C-133 gave Military Airlift Command the ability to move troops to trouble spots around the world. But MAC had more humanitarian duties too, like carrying medical teams to immunise children after floods in Morocco—

—or airlifting United Nations peace-keeping forces to the Congo—

—even a grief-stricken pilgrim, one of 4,000, was safely airlifted to Mecca—

—and the Chilean earthquake disaster of 1960 saw MAC flying in urgently-needed supplies and evacuating the homeless

Even bigger was the Lockheed C-141 Star-Lifter

New bomber aircraft also began to enter service, like this Boeing B-47 Stratojet, seen deploying a braking parachute as it lands

It was followed by the Boeing B-52, most important component of Strategic Air Command's deterrent force, seen carrying two Hound Dog missiles

Flight refuelling from a Boeing KC-135 flying-tanker enables SAC B-52s
to stay in the air for as long as necessary

Flight refuelling techniques were developed to extend the range of all
classes of aircraft, like this heavy helicopter

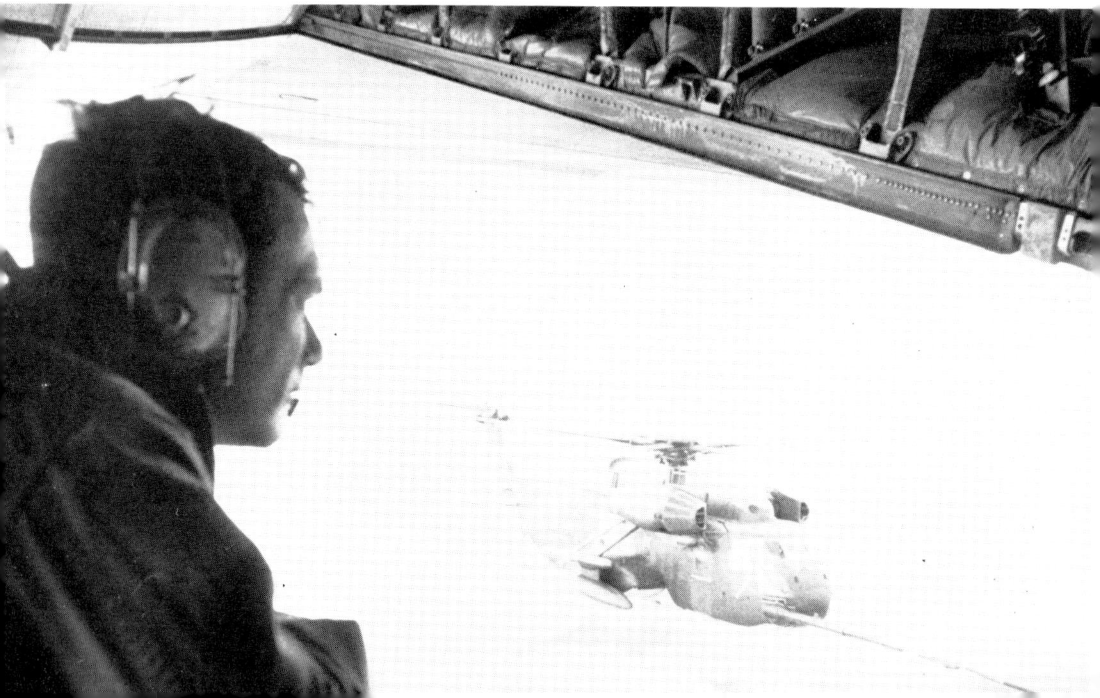

And here a Douglas RB-66 Destroyer approaches the tail drogue of a KB-50 tanker over Europe

Simultaneously with the development of the new generation aircraft came the first of the missiles. The USAF's first bombardment missile was Matador, with simple radio-navigation guidance

It was followed by the 6,000-mile range Snark which could carry a 5,000lb nuclear warhead

First of the USAF's ICBMs was Atlas, seen here at launch—

Matador was replaced eventually by the more advanced Mace, seen here deployed behind the ''Iron Curtain''

—and Thor, also about to leave its launch-pad

Jupiter, being launched from Cape Canaveral, was a contemporary of Thor

First Titan II to be launched from an underground silo climbs away into space

Still from a film sequence shows the first stage of a Titan II ICBM tumbling to Earth, as the second stage accelerates away. Earth's curvature is seen clearly at the top of the picture

A Thor rocket was used to launch the USAF's first Discoverer satellite

Shortly afterwards, a Thor-Able rocket placed the Tiros 1 meteorological satellite into orbit

Important Strategic Air Command deterrent is the Minuteman ICBM, seen here housed in its underground silo

Minuteman climbs and arcs over on to course after silo launch

Film sequence shows Titan II launch from underground silo

The North American X-15 research aircraft climbs away into the night-sky of space

The Convair B-58 Hustler, the USAF's first supersonic bomber, seen on take-off

—it looks even more impressive in the air, with a huge jettisonable pod beneath the slim fuselage

The Boeing Bomarc, —and in the air
surface-to-air interceptor
missile, at launching—

Lockheed YF-12A experimental interceptor fighter, the existence of
which was first announced in 1964. It has a reported top speed in excess
of Mach 3

A Strategic Air Command SR-71 strategic reconnaissance aircraft takes
on fuel from a KC-135 tanker

The need to gain fast information of impending missile or aircraft attack led to the establishment of a worldwide network of early-warning sites. This shows a Ballistic Missile Early Warning Site (BMEWS) at Thule, Greenland

Here is another site, high on a Spanish mountain peak

Texas Tower early warning radar station, some 100 miles off the US Atlantic coastline

Longer radar range is possible from an airborne station, so Lockheed RC-121Cs were equipped to carry some 6 tons of radar and special electronic equipment and a crew of 31 for long-endurance flights

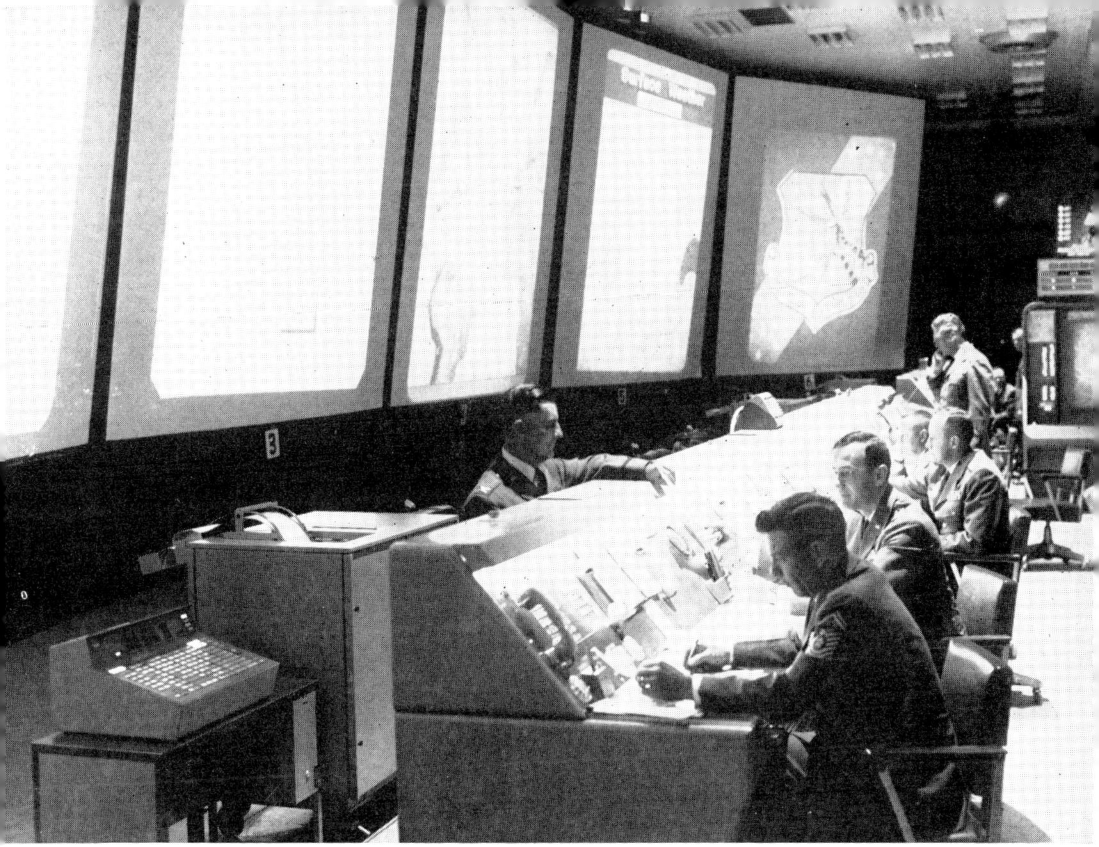

The information gathered from around the world is fed to Strategic Air Command's underground headquarters, where it is monitored 24 hours of every day

This Communications Status Centre ensures the reliability of SAC's worldwide communications systems

In the unlikely event that SAC's headquarters should be eliminated by a nuclear attack, airborne command posts, maintaining permanent watch by overlap of a series of aircraft, are able to take control of all intercontinental-range bombers and missiles

Lower down the scale, a Minuteman combat crew has control of ten silo-stored missiles

Headquarters Strategic Air Command, at Omaha, Nebraska, lies in a peaceful setting. The missile shell on display leaves little doubt, however, of its intention to use any means to maintain or restore worldwide peace

It is useless having advance warning of enemy attack unless your own reaction time is adequate. Frequent exercises ensure this is so, and USAFE crews at a Spanish base race to their F-104s as the alarm sounds

Somewhere in America, an SAC B-52 crew races to their always ready-and-waiting heavy bomber. Note one of the Hound Dog missiles alongside the fuselage

Far away in Britain, RB-66 bomber crews at Alconbury AFB show that they, too, are ready for instant action

No less important in the USAF's peace-keeping task is the ability of Military Air Lift Command and Tactical Air Command to airlift vast numbers of troops and their equipment to any part of the world under all weather conditions

War in Vietnam, remote from the US homeland, has emphasised again the need for vast transport aircraft. MAC and TAC are able to deploy a wide variety, as seen here at Tan Son Nhut airfield near Saigon, with a Boeing C-97 Stratofreighter in the foreground

A Fairchild C-123 Provider manoeuvres along a narrow airstrip at Dan Tieng, Vietnam

Douglas C-124 Globemaster II at Tan Son Nhut: it has a gross take-off weight of 194,500lb

Lockheed C-130 Hercules tactical transport at Tan Son Nhut. The USAF's multi-mission transport aircraft, the C-130, is able to land and take off from front-line airstrips

The Douglas C-133 Cargomaster, here at Tan Son Nhut, is able to transport any of the USAF's IRBMs and ICBMs, and has a maximum take-off weight of 275,000lb

Lockheed C-141 StarLifter seen in Vietnam, is a long-range transport with a gross take-off weight of 323,600lb, and able to carry a Minuteman missile

The Boeing C-135, non-tanker version of the well-known KC-135, is able to carry at least 126 troops or 89,000lb of cargo, and has a ferry range of 9,200 miles

Grandaddy of them all—the Lockheed C-5A Galaxy, now entering MAC service, will carry up to 270 troops, or a military payload of nearly 120 tons

The Boeing-developed flying-boom, here fitted to a KC-97A Stratofreighter, has simplified the task of flight refuelling, which has become a most essential operational technique in Vietnam

92591

Here a KC-135 Stratotanker over Vietnam lowers the refuelling boom—ready to quench the thirst of a B-52 operating from far-distant Guam

F-105 Thunderchiefs queue to refuel from a KC-135 tanker *en route* to targets in North Vietnam

The drogue and probe method of flight refuelling also can be of value. Here a technician checks over the equipment

A Sikorsky HH-3E helicopter approaches the drogue of a Hercules tanker, so extending the search and rescue range of these aircraft

Vietnam has seen the deployment of the USAF's latest aircraft: here F-4C Phantoms drop their bombs under radar control

A McDonnell F-4C Phantom lands in South Vietnam with braking parachute deployed

The F-111 ''swing-wing'' fighter has also served in Vietnam—

—and is shown here with wing fully swept

A Cessna O-1E of a Forward Air Controller dives to pinpoint a Viet Cong concentration—

—then fires a smoke rocket to mark the location for strike aircraft—

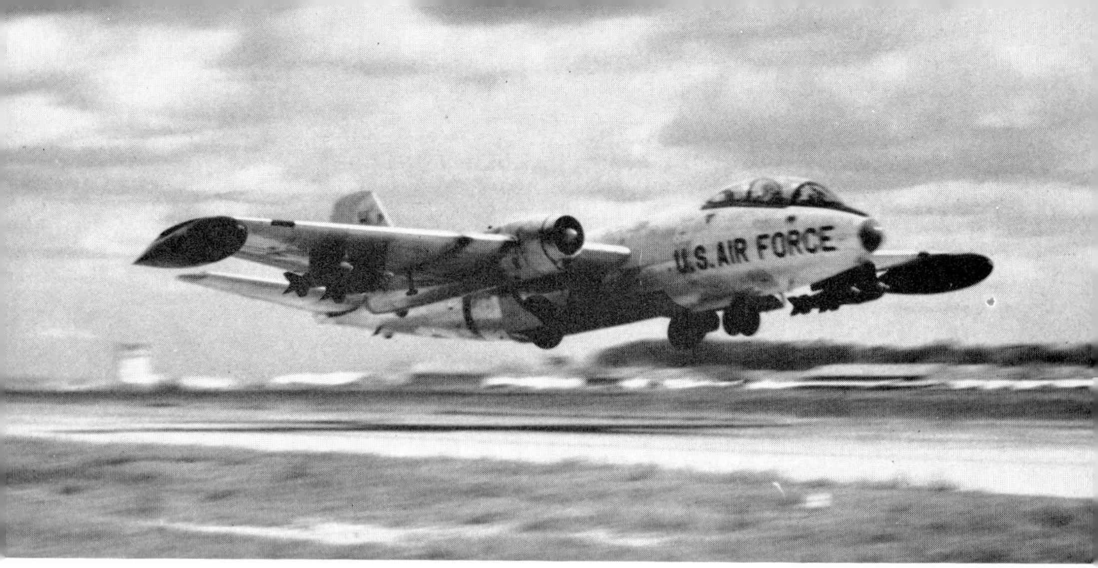
U.S. AIR FORCE

EO
361

EO
272

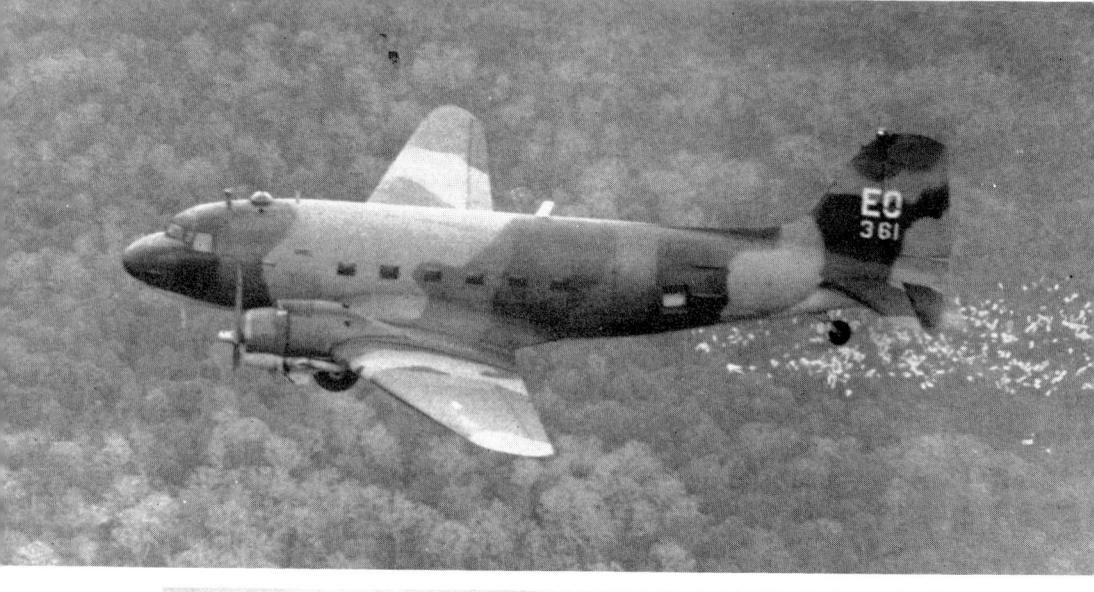

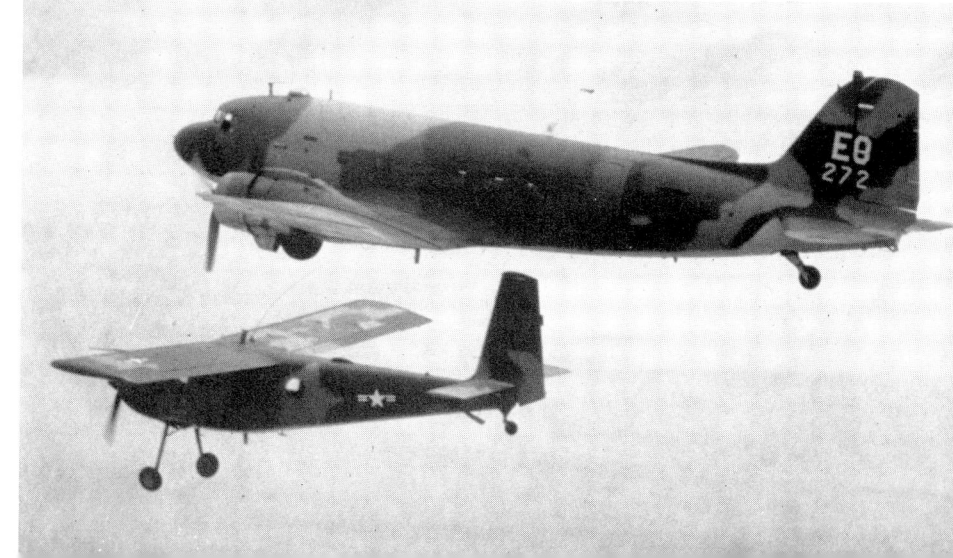

—such as the B-57 Canberra which has been standing at the ready

Psychological tactics have included leaflet dropping from Douglas C-47s, in an effort to induce Viet Cong troops to surrender

Supplies in forward areas not only arrive by helicopter, they are also air dropped as from this C-130 Hercules at Junction City, Tay Ninh Province

"Speaker Bird" (the Helio U-10) and "Sister Gabby" (C-47) operating from Binh Thuy AB drop leaflets and broadcast tape recordings as their contribution to the psychological warfare rôle

This C-123K makes a cargo drop from its rear door

In Vietnam, helicopters have again displayed their unique values. The "Jolly Green Giants" (HH-3Es) retrieving an aircrew member to fight again

An HH-43 Huskie with fire-fighting equipment was on the scene quickly enough to prevent serious damage to this A-1E Skyraider that belly-landed at Da Nang

A USAF HH-43 takes off from its South Vietnam base on a rescue mission

The B-57 Canberra, of British origin, has proved valuable in Vietnam, particularly in the RB-57 reconnaissance version

Even the humble trainer can develop warlike characteristics. Cessna A-37 trainers, redesignated A-37A, served with the 604th Tactical Fighter Squadron at Bien Hoa AB—

—when called upon to harass the Viet Cong—

—they could oblige with a salvo of 38 2·75in rockets

F-105 Thunderchief's *en route* to
strike a target in North Vietnam

This was the sort of target fre-
quently met on the way—a North
Vietnamese MiG-17 photographed
during a dog fight

But this MiG-17 did not live to
fight another day, and very nearly
collided with the Thunderchief
that destroyed it

Lockheed C-141 StarLifters include
among many duties that of air
ambulance, able to carry 80 litter
patients and eight attendants

New specialised medical transport
of MAC, the McDonnell Douglas
C-9A Nightingale, provides hospital ward care for up to 30 litter
patients

Flying under the radar control of
a B-66 Destroyer, F-105 Thunderchiefs bomb North Vietnam
through low cloud cover

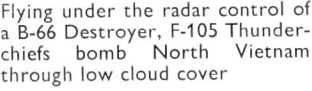

An F-104 Starfighter way above the clouds in Vietnam

Assistance requested by a Forward Air Controller results in a blanket of flame from an exploding phosphorous bomb

On July 21, 1969, Col. Edwin "Buzz" Aldrin clambers down from the lunar module *Eagle*— first USAF officer and second man on the Moon's surface

Here "Buzz" Aldrin stands beside a Solar Wind Composition Experiment—

—and busies himself deploying a Passive Seismic Experiments Package.
Behind stands the lunar module—seemingly frail life-line back to Earth

The late President John F. Kennedy had said that America would put
men on the Moon before 1970. One can but wonder at "Buzz" Aldrin's
thoughts and feelings as he stands on the lunar surface, beside Old
Glory

The first moon landing by astronauts Armstrong and Aldrin might then have been considered hazardous, but their vista was far more peaceful than that of their fellow-servicemen fighting in Vietnam. Right in the front-line was the Forward Air Controller (FAC), the policeman on his beat. As the war progressed, early aircraft which had been adapted for this role were replaced by more specialised types such as this Cessna O-2A

Even more sophisticated was the North American OV-10 Bronco, used for FAC and COIN (counter insurgency) operations. Able to carry a ton and a half of mixed ordnance, its two-man crew had an excellent view of the terrain below, simplifying their search for enemy guerrillas moving through the jungle. Some OV-10As were modified under the USAF's "Pave Nail" programme to equip them for night FAC operations

"Pave Nail" was but one of many USAF code-names covering electronic counter-measures (ECM) and airborne early warning (AEW) systems. "Igloo White" was an ambitious three-element project to pinpoint enemy infiltration. First link was an air-launched sensor, Adsid for example, which buried itself in the ground to leave exposed only an almost invisible antenna. Picking up vibrations from moving vehicles, it transmitted them to an orbiting relay aircraft which, in turn, passed the information to an Infiltration Surveillance Center (ISC), which could then take appropriate action. The big, costly to operate and vulnerable Lockheed EC-121Rs used initially as relay aircraft were replaced, under project "Pave Eagle", by small off-the-shelf Beechcraft Bonanzas designated QU-22B. Specially-equipped for their relay task they were flown usually under remote control, but carried a pilot/observer to monitor the electronic equipment

The ease with which the Vietcong and their allies could infiltrate through the jungle meant that USAF reconnaissance and surveillance aircraft were of prime importance. The most impressive striking force was useless unless you could locate the enemy. This helps explain why Boeing C-135 transports began to lose their sleek lines as they became packed with electronic sensors. Blossoming on noses, fuselages and fins in bewildering variety were advanced infra-red devices sensitive to heat emission, special radar equipment and even "people sniffers", to help in the endless search

Several types of aircraft which had originated for peaceful purposes, like the Beechcraft Bonanza (QU-22B), were called up to add to the USAF's inventory of special duty aircraft. But although many civil and military aircraft were adaptable as "spy planes", some specialised aircraft were needed. Lockheed's SR-71A, still one of the world's fastest aircraft in 1973, proved invaluable to give a broad-scale reconnaissance picture of operations in Southeast Asia

The English Electric Canberra had evolved in Britain soon after the second World War as an advanced and highly manoeuvrable jet bomber. In America, the Glenn L. Martin company began to build them under licence and developed a reconnaissance version. Later, General Dynamics produced an ultra-high-altitude strategic reconnaissance version, the RB-57F illustrated. With the large-area wing spanning 122ft and extended nose for advanced electronics, its parentage is hardly recognisable

Maximum speed of the F-105D was about 1,390mph at 38,000ft, and it had an initial rate of climb approaching $6\frac{1}{2}$ miles per minute. Not surprisingly it was a fuel-thirsty machine, and in-flight refuelling was an essential part of its day-to-day operations

Conflict in Vietnam was very different to that of the two world wars: the confrontations of huge land armies gave place to a sinister and deadly game of hide and seek. When the enemy was located he had to be hit hard and fast, before he could move to two other places. Initially, most of these attacks were made by aircraft like the Republic F-105 Thunderchief, called in to make a strike by the FACs. Illustrated is an F-105D (rear), which had a fully integrated flight and fire control system, and an F-105F fully-operational two-seat mission trainer

Combat aircraft like the F-105D had begun to attain a fairly high degree of sophistication. This view of the cockpit gives some slight appreciation of the very high standard of training needed by the pilots who flew such aircraft as routine. It was a long and difficult trail from the moment of their first solo flight

In 1952 the USAF decided to adopt a jet trainer for primary flight instruction, leading to development of the Cessna T-37, but it was not until 1961 that the Air Force adopted all-through jet training

Evaluation of the new training procedure showed that the T-37, far more costly to operate than a small piston-engined aircraft, was an expensive way of finding out if a particular individual would or would not make the grade. It was decided in July 1964 to revert to a 30-hour primary phase on piston-engined aircraft (reduced to 16 hours in 1971), using the Cessna T-41 Mescalero, followed by 90 hours (82 in 1971) in the T-37

Performance of the T-37 was, of course, a big step from that of the supersonic aircraft which pilots selected for the fighter wings would have to fly. In March of 1961 the USAF's first supersonic trainer, the Northrop T-38A Talon, was handed over to Air Training Command at Randolph AFB, Texas. Capable of a speed of Mach 1.2, many questioned the ability of a pupil to transfer safely from the 400mph plus T-37 to the supersonic T-38. Its success was confirmed ten years later when the training schedules were revised, and at which time Air Training Command had approximately 1,000 of these superb aircraft

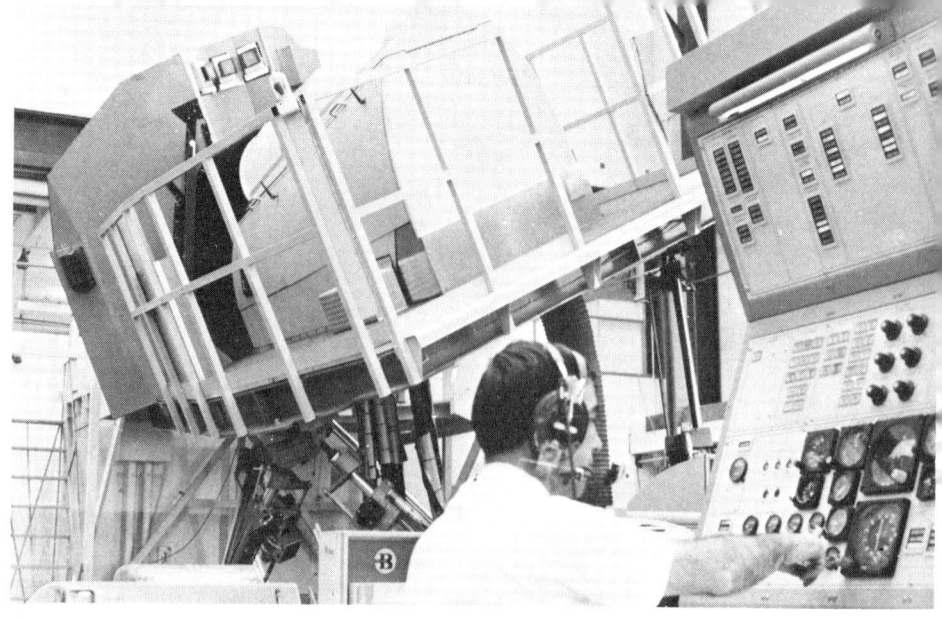

An ability to fly the aeroplane safely, whatever its speed, is not sufficient. Modern combat aircraft are closely integrated weapon systems and the transition from even such an advanced trainer as the T-38 to a McDonnell Douglas F-4 Phantom II is an enormous step. Its accomplishment is made easier by the use of sophisticated flight simulators like this Singer F-4D weapon system trainer, the interior of the trainer complex presenting a faithful replica of the F-4D cockpit. In it the pilot learns not only to fly the Phantom, but how best to use its communication, navigation, ECM and weapon launching systems. When he sits in the real aeroplane he is immediately at home

The Phantom II was developed initially to meet a US Navy requirement for a long-range all-weather attack fighter (AH-1). The USAF made an almost unprecedented decision to adopt the fighter for Air Force service with only marginal changes. The definitive F-4E version had a 20mm forward-firing multi-barrel cannon, and could carry Sparrow or Sidewinder air-to-air missiles or up to 16,000lb of mixed ordnance. Illustrated is the RF-4C, a reconnaissance version which has side-looking radar, infra-red detectors and forward- and side-looking cameras

With increasing experience of operations in Vietnam, the USAF considered that an armed version of the T-37 trainer would prove valuable for close support, armed reconnaissance and FAC duties. A far cry from the 1,500mph Phantom II, a squadron of A-37As was evaluated in Vietnam, leading to production of the A-37B with more powerful engines, in-flight refuelling capability and other improvements. Cessna's little machine, armed with a 7·62mm multi-barrel Minigun and able to carry 5,000lb of mixed ordnance, packed a hefty punch

The A-37s proved valuable in dealing with enemy combat troops moving forward into South Vietnam, freeing more sophisticated aircraft for the task of hitting strategic targets in the North. Their success suggested that the heavy workload on primary combat aircraft could be relieved still more in the South by introducing gunship versions of old piston-engined transport aircraft. Possessing long endurance and the capacity for a large load of equipment, sensors, guns and ammunition, aircraft like this Fairchild AC-119K did yeoman service in this role

An interior shot of the AC-119K gunship shows clearly what excellent gun platforms they made, with plenty of space and adequate headroom for the gunners

Following the precedent established in adopting the Navy's F-4 Phantom II, the USAF evinced interest in the Vought Corsair II. Evolved as a carrier-based subsonic fighter able to lift a heavy weapon load, an A-7D tactical fighter version was ordered for the USAF. Able to carry over 15,000lb of mixed ordnance, including air-to-air and air-to-ground missiles, the A-7D has an advanced continuous-solution navigation and weapon delivery system, giving a capability of all-weather radar bomb delivery

One of the most controversial aircraft to enter USAF service was the General Dynamics F-111. The requirement was for an aeroplane able to operate from short and rough airfields, with supersonic low level speed, Mach 2 plus performance at altitude and unrefuelled ferry range across the Atlantic or Pacific. To meet the very differing slow-speed landing and take-off and high-speed combat requirements, a variable-geometry wing configuration was adopted. When the first six F-111As entered service in Southeast Asia, three were lost within four weeks and Congress raised a loud voice. USAF planning was proved right, and towards the end of the Vietnam War F-111As of the 474th Tactical Fighter Wing proved so effective that single aircraft could be deployed against airfields, SAM sites and priority targets in all weather by day or night. Illustrated is an F-111F with improved avionics and more powerful engines

Vital in the strategic bomber role has been the B-52 which pounded targets in North Vietnam until the cease-fire in early 1973, and a B-52D is shown in night camouflage. Although the type first became operational in 1955, it is still a significant weapon in Strategic Air Command's inventory in 1973, and large numbers are being adapted to carry 20 Short Range Attack Missiles (SRAMs)

Military Airlift Command has the enormous job of logistic support and aeromedical evacuation. A difficult task under the best conditions, it is aggravated to an extreme when the support line stretches half way around the world. Early mainstay for operations in Southeast Asia was the Lockheed C-141A StarLifter. Equipped with an all-weather landing system, it can accommodate 154 troops, 123 paratroops, 80 litters and 16 sitting casualties, or lift 70,847lb of freight over a range of 4,080 miles

A need to supplement the lift capability of the C-141 was soon apparent to Military Airlift Command, leading to development of the Lockheed C-5A Galaxy. This became another controversial aeroplane due to escalating production costs. Nonetheless, its value has been well proven in the Vietnam War, demonstrating great reliability with 112,600lb payloads carried over a range of 6,333 miles

While the monster transports could play a vital casualty-evacuation role, Military Airlift Command appreciated the need for a more specialised aircraft to equip its 375th Aeromedical Wing. This led to the C-9A Nightingale, basically a McDonnell Douglas DC-9 Series 30 civil transport. It differs in interior configuration, equipped to carry 30 to 40 litter patients, with two nurses and three aeromedical technicians in attendance, and has also an intensive-care compartment. Two of its three entrance doors have hydraulically-operated stairways, the third a hydraulically operated ramp to simplify the loading of litters

The Korean War had first demonstrated the important contribution that rotary-winged aircraft could make to combat operations. When the USAF were committed to conflict in Vietnam they could benefit by the availability of improved helicopters. A Sikorsky CH-3C is seen uplifting a 105mm field gun for delivery to an Army outpost

Another requirement was for a helicopter able to patrol near the North Vietnam border to provide a rescue service for any combat crews shot down over enemy-held territory. Sikorsky HH-53s with jettisonable auxiliary fuel tanks, flight refuelling probe, armour, armament, all-weather avionics and rescue hoist were ordered for the Aerospace Rescue and Recovery Service

Drones have been in service with armed forces for years, usually operated as targets for the training of anti-aircraft gunners. New developments in electronics made it possible to design reconnaissance drones that could take a close look at targets which might hazard the crew of a more conventional reconnaissance aircraft. This Lockheed DC-130 "mother plane" is setting out on a mission to launch and control its clutch of four RPVs

The Air Force Systems Command has an unenviable task of gazing into a crystal ball, trying to evolve the best possible defensive and offensive force for the future. As a new navigational trainer it has selected the T-43A, a special version of the Boeing 737 civil transport. Beginning to enter service in 1973, each can carry 12 students, four advanced students and three instructors

Aircraft deployed on the airborne early-warning command-and-control role are of vital importance. To enhance this capability the Air Force is acquiring a new Airborne Warning and Control System (AWACS) aircraft, based on the Boeing 707. This EC-137D prototype has an advanced downward-looking radar housed in its large rotating dorsal radome

To maintain a combat potential better than that of any likely enemy, Air Force Systems Command initiated development of an air superiority fighter. With powerful turbofan engines to give it a thrust-to-weight ratio of better than one-to-one, and emphasis on manoeuvrability, rate of climb and acceleration rather than high-speed high-altitude capability, the McDonnell Douglas F-15A Eagle was in production for Tactical Air Command in 1973. New ''dogfight'' versions of the Sidewinder missile and a newly-developed multi-barrel cannon will give it immense destructive power at close range

Neither has the USAF forgotten entirely the potential of aircraft able to travel in space. A joint programme with NASA has produced the newly-configured lifting-body research aircraft designated X-24B. Completely rebuilt by Martin Marietta from the earlier X-24A, this made its first unpowered flight on August 1st, 1973 launched from a B-52 ''mother-plane''. There seems little doubt that the, USAF is becoming equipped superbly, and that its deterrent potential has retained its significance. The primary task of the USAF is that of a world-wide peace-keeping force: a role which it is determined to maintain regardless of the expense